Words West

GINGER WADSWORTH

CLARION BOOKS ✦ NEW YORK

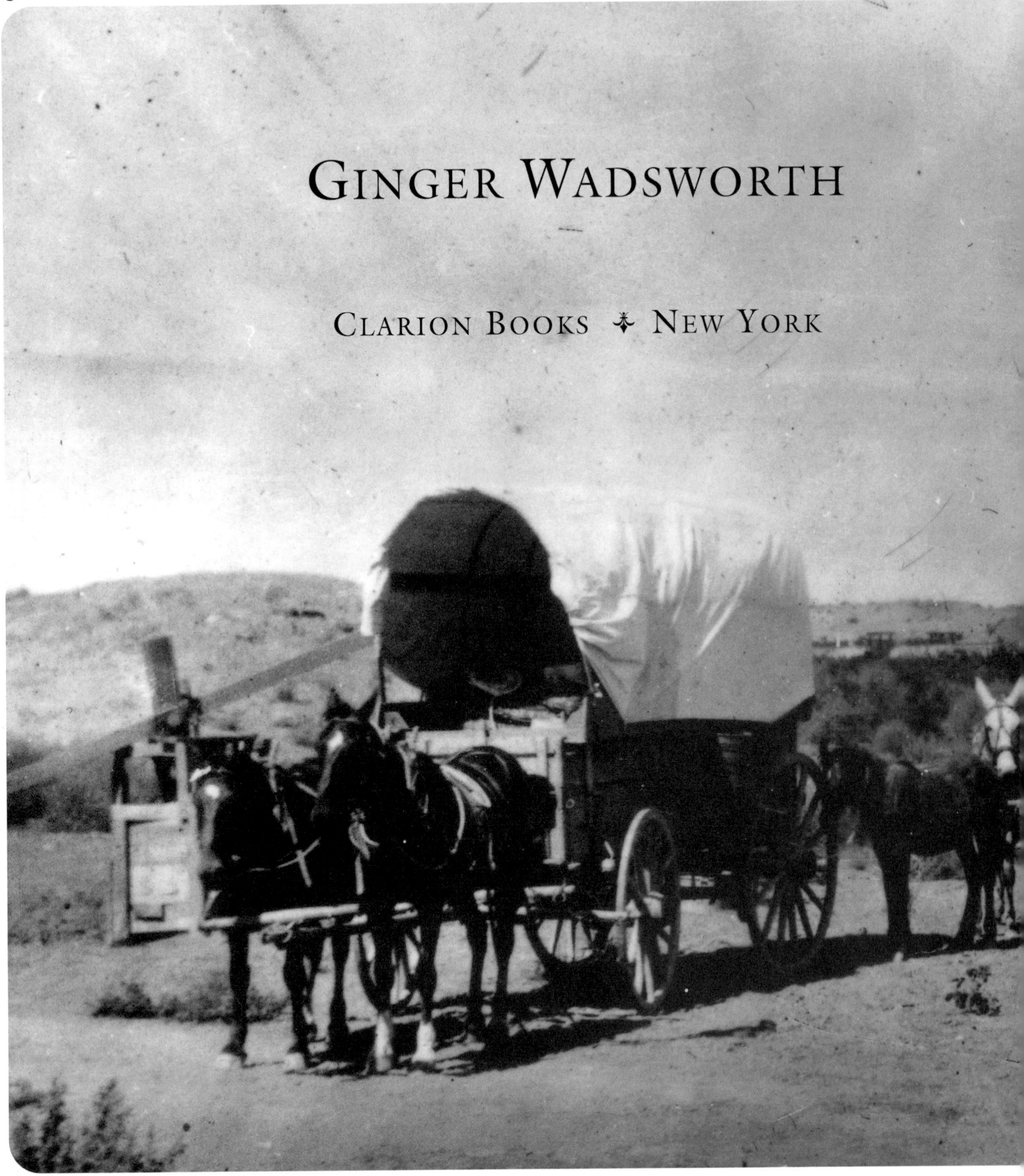

Words West

Voices of Young Pioneers

Clarion Books
a Houghton Mifflin Company imprint
215 Park Avenue South, New York, NY 10003
Copyright © 2003 by Ginger Wadsworth

The text was set in 12-point Galliard.

www.houghtonmifflinbooks.com

Printed in the U.S.A.

Photograph on title page and page 96 used by permission of Sharlot Hall Museum. (Photograph by
Clark Vieter.) Photograph on pages 153 and 192–93 used by permission of Department of
Special Collections, Stanford University Libraries.

The following list of known illustration numbers is provided in accordance with the terms of applicable
agreements required by permission holders:

Arizona Historical Society, p. 134: AHS1927; *The Bancroft Library*, p. 56: 1903:17175:143; p. 93: ffF580P455;
Brigham Young University, jacket & p. 28: 30695; p. 67: 328; p. 104: 663; *Colorado Historical Society*, p. 125: F3975;
Denver Public Library, p. 34: Z-121; p. 38: Z-329; p. 45: X-11929; p. 47: F-22781; p. 73: F-6778; p. 78: F-247;
p. 123: F-24574; p. 127: F-13339; p. 135: Z-308; p. 143: Z-223; p. 144: K-218; *The Huntington Library*, p. 30:
PhotPF1548; p. 35: HM8044#19; p. 55: HM8044#87; p. 85: AP2H3 Vol.39; p. 117: HM8044#18; p. 122:
PhotCL312(276); p. 162: HM16994; *Idaho State Historical Society*, p. 7: 65.128.38; *Missouri Historical Society*, jacket
& p. 138: 1961.75.1; p. 18: 1961.73.3; p. 111: P82.28.1; p. 124: *Harper's Weekly*, May 1874; p. 128: #90, Perry
Collection; *Museum of New Mexico*, p. 2: 15069; p. 40: 3083; p. 42: 65054; p. 79: 8191; p. 148: 70437; *Nebraska State
Historical Society*, p. 70: RG2608-2938A; p. 119: RG3351-8; *New-York Historical Society* p. 68: 2000.436; p. 89:
52537; *Oregon Historical Society*, p. 8: OrHi637; p. 24: OrHi86607; p. 52: OrHi86985; p. 147: OrHi35576; p. 156:
OrHi80278; p. 158: OrHi553; *Smithsonian Institution, NAA* p. 107: 1668; p. 109: 76-13355; *Southern Oregon
Historical Society*, p. 19: 726; *State Historical Society of Wisconsin*, p. 48: WHi3935; *University of Wyoming, AHC*,
p. 102: Throssel#439

Library of Congress Cataloging-in-Publication Data

Wadsworth, Ginger.
Words west : voices of young pioneers / Ginger Wadsworth.
p. cm.
Contents: Opening the West—Preparations and leaving home—Jumping off—Hoping to go twenty
miles in a day—Oregon or bust—California gold and other destinations—Entertainment and
celebrations—Chores and chow—Life, death, and accidents—Indians—Mother nature rules—
Dry and hot—Over mountains—The ever-changing trail and times.
ISBN 0-618-23475-6
1. Pioneer children—West (U.S.)—History—19th century—Juvenile literature. 2. Pioneer children—
West (U.S.)—Biography—Juvenile literature. 3. Frontier and pioneer life—West (U.S.)—Juvenile
literature. 4. Overland journeys to the Pacific—Juvenile literature. 5. West (U.S.)—History—
19th century—Juvenile literature. 6. West (U.S.)—Biography—Juvenile literature.
[1. Pioneers. 2. Overland journeys to the Pacific. 3. Overland Trails.
4. Frontier and pioneer life—West (U.S.) 5. West (U.S.)—History.] I. Title.
F596.W24 2003
917.804'2'083—dc21
2003003764

VB 10 9 8 7 6 5 4 3 2 1

In memory of
W. Turrentine Jackson (1915–2000),
History Professor at the University of California at Davis.
Thanks, "Turpie," for teaching us Western American History
with such gusto!

Contents

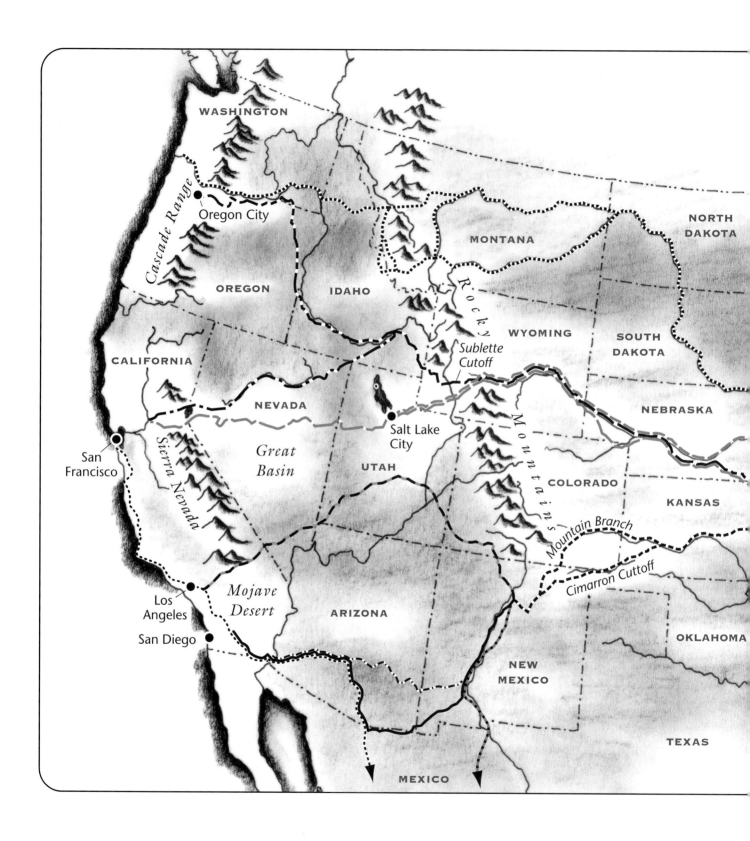

MAJOR TRAILS WEST

Oregon-California Trail   — — — — —

Oregon Trail   —·—·—·—

California Trail   —··—··—··—

Mormon Trail   – – – – –

Lewis & Clark Trail   ·················

Pony Express Route   — — — —

Santa Fe Trail   - - - - - - - -

Southern Trail   ──────────

Gila Trail   –·–·–·–·–·

Old Spanish Trail   — — — — —

El Camino Real   ▬▬▬▬▬▬

Anza Trail   ···············

Map shows current state boundaries.

IOWA

Council Bluffs

Nauvoo

Independence

MISSOURI

ARKANSAS

Pioneers traveled in whatever kind of wagon they had or could afford. With their white tops, these prairie schooners looked like a fleet of ships sailing across a sea of grass.
(AUTHOR'S PHOTO, SCOTTS BLUFF NATIONAL MONUMENT, NEBRASKA)

Author's Note

Cook beans and coffee over an open fire of sagebrush or buffalo chips.

Wear the same *dress* for six months.

Sleep in a new place every night.

Leave my friends forever.

No way!

I learned a lot about pioneer life during the summer I turned twelve. That's when my parents took a family vacation to explore the American West. During the summer, we traveled thousands of miles. We visited forts, battlefields, and ghost towns. My mother had us walk beside the wheel ruts of the Oregon Trail. At Sutter's Fort in California, we tried panning for gold and failed. We peered into prairie schooners and watched docents reenact historical events. The car sped across the seemingly endless desert, took bridges over rivers, and zigzagged up and down mountain passes.

Besides stopping to read each historical marker, we detoured on bumpy dirt roads to explore ghost towns and rundown cemeteries on lonely-looking slopes. As we drove, my father filled us with historical details and spellbinding tales about the "wild west." He also told us about the forty thousand children, from infants to teenagers, who accompanied their families on great overland journeys to the West between 1840 and 1870.

Years later, I had forgotten most of the dates and details but still thought of those young pioneers. Why did they leave? How did they feel? I wondered. Didn't they miss their friends and relatives? How did they know what routes to take? What did they do about school? These questions and others flooded my mind.

I began to read journals, letters, and reminiscences of people who journeyed west. Most trail diaries were written quickly, to capture the moment, and with little regard for spelling and grammar. Some were sad; others were funny. I read about one pioneer who apologized to his diary for his "inklings" as "I write seated upon a bucket, with a board on my knees, a candle in a lantern, wind blowing, and extremely cold." Some reminiscences were recorded years later, often for grandchildren or for local historical societies.

My father and grandfather, both named Hal G. Evarts, wrote about

Thousands of people carved their names on Register Cliff near the North Platte River in Wyoming. (AUTHOR'S PHOTO)

the West. I own copies of their published books and inherited many of the books that they used for research. In bookstores and via the Internet, I browsed and bought old and new books related to western history. Family vacations, with my sons, paralleled those trips I made with my parents. At Register Cliff in Wyoming, where thousands of emigrants carved their names in the soft sandstone, I found this inscription: *J. T. Wadsworth, 1859*. A relative, perhaps?

Without realizing it, I was preparing my mind for the fulfillment of a lifelong dream. My writing, both published and unpublished, has often focused on the West and on young pioneers such as Marion Russell, who traveled on the Santa Fe Trail in 1852 at the age of seven, and Laura Ingalls Wilder. But at some point, it was time to "put pen to paper" and write *Words West: Voices of Young Pioneers*.

Generally, the young people I've included in this book were teenagers. But some were only toddlers, like three-year-old Eliza Donner, and others were young adults. John Bidwell was twenty-one when he started west. Back then, children grew up quickly. Every child had a job. Whatever their age, they were expected to work hard. Young married women—many still teenagers—came west, often with a child or expecting one along the way. Older teenage boys were considered adults. They carried guns and, like sixteen-year-old Edward Lenox, could cast votes related to a wagon train's decisions along the way.

The journals gave me great admiration for my ancestors, and yours, who wanted to make a new and better start in life. For the most part, I have not tinkered with their writing or spelling.

Here's how it all began for these young travelers.

Chapter One

OPENING THE WEST

I [saw] a look on dear mother's face that I had never seen before. I walked away after the usual greeting and sat silent. After a time [Mother's] voice strengthened and she said, 'what do you think your father has done. . . . He has sold the farm and as soon as school closes we are to move.'"

Sarah Cummins, a young bride and a farmer's daughter, had just come into the family home when she heard these words. Sarah was excited about going to Oregon. It was hard to raise crops in the over-farmed Missouri soil. Her family didn't have enough to eat, and her mother was often sick. Sunny weather and rich farm soil at the end of the trail sounded like paradise to sixteen-year-old Sarah.

Good farmland was the most common cause for moving west. But there were other reasons why people "hit the trail" with their families and belongings. Sallie Hester's family left because Sallie's father was "going in search of health."

Some went west for gold. But after the peak in 1852, most of California's easy-to-find gold was gone. Thirteen-year-old Harriet

Hitchcock's family wanted to strike it rich, but in the newly discovered gold fields of Colorado. When Harriet started her diary on June 2, 1864, she was facing the setting sun, with the wagon tongue pointed in the same direction.

> And what is the harm in simply penning a few thoughts now and then by the way side or by the side of the way, for it is a new and strange way that we are going to travel. Well . . . here we are . . . camping out. We have two wagons. . . . This new mode of life seems very strange . . . as I gaze for miles on the rolling prairie.

Slaves and free blacks also traveled on the trails. So did white families who wanted to escape the oppressive world of slavery. During the late 1830s, thousands of American settlers were welcomed into the north-

A wagon was a family's only home for months. The rectangular-shaped wagon box was about eight to ten feet long. Waterproof canvas, which was stretched over stout wooden hoops, protected the family's belongings.
(MUSEUM OF NEW MEXICO)

ern Mexican province of Tejas, which later became the state of Texas. First, they had to swear allegiance to Mexico and its government.

Members of the Church of Jesus Christ of Latter-day Saints, or Mormons, fled west to escape religious persecution in Illinois and Missouri. They settled in the Great Salt Lake Valley, in what later become the state of Utah. In 1863, a Mormon traveler wrote:

> [St. Joseph, Missouri] is the gathering place for those [of us] who intend to cross the plains [to Salt Lake City]. Their tents were scattered over the hills, and when the camp fires were lit up at night the scene was beautiful to behold. It makes me think how the children of Israel must have looked in the days of Moses, when journeying in the wilderness.

Earlier, in the 1700s, the West was a great untraveled prize. There were rumors of its hidden treasures: woolly mammoths on the prairie, erupting volcanoes, mountains made of salt, and a big river that connected the Atlantic and Pacific Oceans.

President Thomas Jefferson completed the Louisiana Purchase in 1803, adding five hundred million acres to the United States between the Mississippi River and the Rocky Mountains. Immediately, Jefferson sent Meriwether Lewis and William Clark to explore this wilderness area that he had bought from France.

The Lewis and Clark Expedition did not find woolly mammoths or mountains of salt. And they never found a river linking the Pacific and Atlantic Oceans because one does not exist. But the two explorers and their crew traced the Missouri and Columbia Rivers and crossed the Rocky Mountains to the Pacific Ocean and came back.

Everyone on the expedition who could write kept a journal. Americans eagerly read accounts of this historic trip, including William Clark's descriptions of the open country along the Missouri River, "as beautiful as the eye can reach," with wide tree-lined river bottoms. He

Sacajawea, a Shoshone Indian, helped guide Lewis and Clark west. Painting by Alfred Russell.
(MISSOURI HISTORICAL SOCIETY)

added that he and his men "can scarcely cast our eyes in any direction without perceiving deer, elk, buffalo, or antelopes." During their two-year-long journey, the explorers also wrote about western Indian tribes, collected plant and animal specimens, and sketched maps. These words, and their bold trip, attracted the attention of other men.

Some were already in the Northwest, trading with Indians, exploring, or trapping animals for their furs. They came from the United States, Great Britain, France, and other countries. It wasn't crowded. But slowly, by boat, horse, or on foot, more young men left home, following Lewis and Clark's routes. After casting aside homespun farm clothes for buckskin pants and shirts, they took their knives, rifles, and farming skills into the woods to seek adventure. Most never returned to farm life.

These young people became mountain men. Most trapped beaver and other animals up and down the streams and rivers in the mountains. Some preferred to trade instead of trap and bought furs from the Indians. The animal pelts and skins were made into fur hats and coats in the East and in Europe.

There were three types of trappers. Some were hired by organizations like the Rocky Mountain Fur Company. Other skin trappers, as they were also called, worked on credit and paid off their debt to the fur companies at the end of the year. The third group consisted of free trappers who worked alone or in small groups, selling their furs to the highest bidders. Trapping animals in icy-cold streams and rivers, they soon learned, was just as hard as farm work.

Some mountain men could read; others could not. To survive in the wilderness, they had to know how to repair guns, camouflage a cache

TO
Enterprising Young Men.

THE subscriber wishes to engage ONE HUN-
DRED MEN, to ascend the river Missouri
to its source, there to be employed for one, two
or three years.—For particulars, enquire of Major Andrew Henry, near the Lead Mines, in the
County of Washington, (who will ascend with,
and command the party) or to the subscriber at
St. Louis.

Wm. H. Ashley.

February 13   ——98 tf

An 1822 newspaper ad lured Jim Beckwourth, Jim Bridger, James Clyman, Jedediah Smith, and other young men into the West, where they became mountain men and trappers.
(MISSOURI HISTORICAL SOCIETY)

of food supplies and furs, treat wounds, and cure any illnesses—or die. When Jim Bridger was mauled by a grizzly bear, he had his scalp stitched back on his head by another mountain man, without any anesthesia.

Some mountain men felt superior to the Indians they encountered and considered them savages. However, it was important to get along with the various tribes and helpful to learn one or more native language. Jim Beckwourth, a trapper, wrote this statement, which reflected the times but is considered racist in tone today:

> Though the Indian could never become a white man, the white man lapsed easily into an Indian. The mountain man's eye [was] forever watching for the movement of boughs or grasses, for the passage of wild life downwind, something unexplained floating in a stream. . . . His ear . . . was tuned to catch any sound in a country where every sound was provisionally a death warning. He dressed like an Indian, in blankets, robes, buckskins, and moccasins. . . . He lived like an Indian in bark huts or skin lodges, and married a succession of squaws. He had on call a brutality as instant as the Indian's and rather more relentless.

As they trapped, the mountain men not only learned about the land and the Indian tribes, but about animals and plants. They discovered natural highways across the North American continent through great river valleys, across prairies, and over mountain passes. This knowledge influenced future travelers.

Missionaries were the first to follow the routes of the mountain men west, to places where they planned to farm and to convert Indian tribes to Christianity. Earlier groups, including Protestant missionaries from the United States and Catholics from France, had already come by ship to Oregon Territory.

One group of missionaries, made up of men and women and led by Marcus Whitman, traveled overland in 1836 to Oregon Country (called Oregon Territory starting in 1846). They settled in the Pacific

Northwest. They hoped to help establish United States claims to the land and encourage settlers to come west.

Whitman, who was a doctor and a Presbyterian missionary, came west with his bride, Narcissa, and another young couple. A second group followed in 1838, proving that both men and women could survive a long wagon journey. An Oregon newspaper noted, "Six white women . . . have already crossed the prairies. . . . And we are assured by their own testimony that they were in better health and spirits at the end than at the beginning of their journey, having found it extremely pleasant. . . . This shows, we think, the feasibility of this route for ladies, and even children."

The timing was perfect! Now farmers and tradespeople knew they could take their families with them by wagon. They headed for the

Nancy Osborn, who came to the Whitman Mission as a child, drew this sketch of the mission from memory as an adult.

Pacific coast, not for the lands between the high plains and the Rocky Mountains. That land was Indian territory. Explorers Lewis and Clark, the mountain men, and others had helped to lay out the possible routes.

The United States headed into a severe economic depression in the late 1830s, followed by a severe drought. Another depression hit in 1841. Banks closed, and no one had much money. It was tough to grow enough food in the worn-out soil. Farmers were losing their land because they couldn't sell their produce or pay their bills.

Many farmers and tradesmen, especially in the Midwest, wanted to move, hoping to build a new life for themselves and their children. They were tired of the long winters when snow buried farms and towns. And all the best land in the Midwest was already taken.

Some people left home because of disease. Malaria was common in the Midwest states along river valleys east of the Mississippi River. Back then, no one knew that malaria was transmitted by mosquitoes. Cholera, another infectious disease, took many other lives in frequent epidemics in eastern cities. When a family member grew sick, the entire family suffered. Each person's help was important. Doctors were few and far between, and in the hard economic times most families didn't have the one to five dollars it took to pay for a doctor's visit anyway.

By 1840, some Americans wanted the United States to expand all the way to the Pacific Ocean, believing that it was the country's "manifest destiny." Restless men in Missouri and other midwestern areas listened to trappers, explorers, and missionaries boast about the beauty of California and Oregon.

Farmers read in newspapers like the *Saint Louis Weekly* that California had "a perpetual spring . . . without the sultriness of summer or the chilling winds of winter . . . a soil unsurpassed for richness and productiveness . . . immense herds of wild cattle . . . woodland[s] and water privileges. . . . [California is] a prize." Others believed that if large numbers of American families settled in Oregon, Great Britain would give up its claim to the western lands below the fifty-fourth parallel in what is now northwestern Canada.

In 1841, the Bidwell-Bartleson Party started out in wagons. This was the first party that didn't consist of trappers or missionaries, but was an organized group of families—thirty-five men, five women, and ten children. They had one thing in common. They were all poor. One man started with seventy-five cents in his pocket. Together, the travelers barely had a hundred dollars among them, but they dreamed of making their fortunes by farming in the West.

John Bidwell, a schoolteacher from Missouri and one of the leaders, admitted that he had a bad case of "California fever." He later penned in his diary, "Our ignorance of the road was complete. We knew that

JAMES K. POLK'S PRESIDENCY

James K. Polk campaigned with slogans such as "Annex Texas" and "Occupy Oregon." During his single term as president from 1845 to 1849, more land was added to the United States than in any other administration except that of Thomas Jefferson, who served as president from 1801 to 1809.

Under Polk, Texas joined the United States as the twenty-eighth state in 1845. Polk threatened Great Britain over the Pacific Northwest. Ultimately, Great Britain backed off from its claims to what would become the future states of Idaho, Washington, Oregon, and parts of Wyoming and Montana.

The United States went to war with Mexico in 1846. The Mexican War ended on February 2, 1848, with the signing of the Treaty of Guadalupe Hidalgo. The United States acquired what would become California, Arizona, Utah, and Nevada and parts of New Mexico, Colorado, and Wyoming.

James Polk's aggressive actions helped to open the Far West to everyday settlers. Most of them didn't think about the many Indian tribes who lived in what was then known as Oregon Territory or about what would happen to them.

This 1844 campaign poster helped elect James K. Polk as the eleventh president of the United States.
(James K. Polk Memorial Association)

California lay west, and that was the extent of our knowledge." They followed the Platte River, reaching Fort John (now called Fort Laramie) and then South Pass in the Rocky Mountains. Most of the travelers had never seen the Rockies before and were surprised by how high and rugged they were.

The group divided in present-day Idaho. Some emigrants took the easier road to Oregon. The remainder, thirty-one men, one woman, and one child, turned west into the unknown and crossed the desert and mountains to reach California. The brutally hot desert was dry and barren, except for sagebrush and prickly cactus. Ahead loomed more mountains, cold and icy even in the summer.

Seventeen-year-old Nancy Kelsey was the only woman in the group, but this didn't bother her. "Where my husband goes, I go." Nancy and her infant daughter, Ann, were the first white females to reach California in an overland emigrant party. The journey took six months.

Following the Bidwell-Bartleson Party's trip, the migration of farming families began in earnest. Some families had owned land that they were leaving behind. Other families had been living out of wagons for years, staying in one place just long enough to raise a season of crops before moving on. Sometimes they were called "movers" by their peers, because they were naturally restless.

Farmers wanted rich farmland, especially land that might be free to the taker in Oregon and other western areas. They hoped to improve their fortunes or their health. California had warm weather and good soil, but it belonged to Mexico. Not everyone was like John Bidwell, who became a Mexican citizen in order to get a large land grant from the Mexican government.

Oregon, however, was another story. President James K. Polk said in his 1845 inaugural address, "Our title to the country of the Oregon is clear and unquestionable." Polk was protesting British claims to the area. He never considered that the land might belong to the various

Indian tribes who had lived there for hundreds of years. Along with other leaders, Polk believed that if American families settled there and farmed the land, they would force out the British.

Before James Polk had even been sworn in as president, many men began selling their farms or businesses to look for better opportunities—usually by moving west. "The motive . . . [in Oregon] was to obtain from the government of United States a grant of land that 'Uncle Sam' had promised to give to the head of each family who settled in this new country," noted one pioneer.

By 1845, "Oregon fever" had truly arrived. Finally the West was open for the large-scale migration of men, women, and children.

Chapter Two

PREPARATIONS AND LEAVING HOME

Lucy Ann Henderson was surprised to learn that she was moving to Oregon. She was at a boarding school in Liberty, Missouri, when "in the spring of '46 my father came for me and took me out of school, to my deep regret. . . .When I got home my parents told me they were going to Oregon. When father lost his farm he decided to go where he could have all the land he wanted for the taking."

At that time, the legal head of each family was a man. Women and children had little, if any, voice in the decision making. Most wives feared the journey west, far from churches, schools, and relatives, but they knew that without a husband or sons around to help, they couldn't run the farm or support themselves.

Ten-year-old William Thompson clearly remembered a spring afternoon in 1852 when "a gentleman came to our house, and after dinner he and my father rode over the [farm]. The next morning, they rode . . . to the county seat. Returning in the evening, my father announced that the [farm] was sold."

The Thompson family began to prepare for the six-month-long trip.

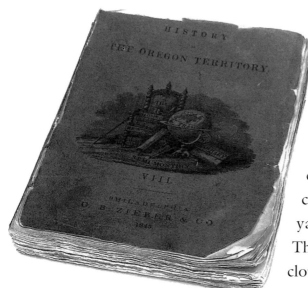

Popular books and magazines help inspire some pioneers to plan their trips and head west.
(AUTHOR'S COLLECTION)

Nearly everything was homespun, including clothes. For farm families, "boughten" cloth was too expensive and not readily available until after the Civil War.

William recalled that, first, "wool [was] carded and spun into thread for [the] old wooden loom." This took a full two weeks. Then it was woven into cloth. Almost every day that spring, William heard the crank of the loom. A family of four needed about forty yards of wool and linen cloth. For the William Thompson family, "The cloth was . . . fashioned into . . . clothing to last a year after we should reach our goal far out on the Pacific shores."

Mothers and daughters cut and fit dresses, as well as shirts and pants for the men and boys. It took a long time because everything was stitched by hand. The sewing machine wouldn't become common until the 1860s. The women stitched undershirts and drawers for the males in the family. Women and girls wore drawers, too, and chemises. Then the females in the family knit shawls, socks, mittens, and caps for winter.

The Scott family decided to go to Oregon in 1852. Thirteen-year-old Kit Scott, one of nine children in her family, wrote about the

> fingers of the women and girls all the winter, providing . . . bedding, blankets, of stockings and sunbonnets, of hickory shirts and gingham aprons . . . that the family might be outfitted for the trip. Ah! The tears that fell upon these garments, fashioned with trembling fingers by the flaring light of tallow candles; the heartaches that were stitched and knitted and woven into them, through the brief winter afternoons.

Other households were just as busy. Eighteen-year-old Sarah Ide, a farmer's daughter in Illinois, helped her family get ready to leave during the winter of 1844–45. One of the many things she did was sew

SOME NECESSITIES FOR THE JOURNEY WEST*

FOOD FOR 3 PEOPLE:

600 pounds of bacon
75 pounds of rice
50 pounds of lard
150 pounds of sugar
50 pounds of dried fruit
10 pounds saleratus [baking soda]
5 barrels of flour = 1,080 pounds
50 pounds of salt and pepper

MISCELLANEOUS:

bedding
1 tent
1 comb
1 brush
3 towels
2 toothbrushes
3 pounds of laundry soap
matches
sewing items
cooking utensils
50 pounds of candles and soap

WEAPONS FOR 1 MAN:

3 rifles
1 belt knife
30 pounds of lead
3 pairs pistols or 2 revolvers
25 pounds of gunpowder

CLOTHING FOR 1 MAN:

1 pair of boots
1 overcoat
1 coat
4 colored silk handkerchiefs
2 pairs stout walking shoes
2 blue or red overshirts
4 pair of woolen socks
1 broad-brimmed hat
2 pairs cotton drawers [undergarment with
    legs, for the lower half of the body]
2 woolen undershirts
1 gutta-percha [waterproof] poncho
2 pairs of cotton socks

*Based on Joseph Ware's The Emigrants' Guide to California, published in 1849.

Ware did not mention that women needed to bring cotton dresses, aprons, and bonnets, plus a shawl or coat. Girls wore simple dresses and aprons, handed down from sister to sister. Their brothers had sturdy pants and shirts, also handed down. Along the way, the women mended and knit socks and mittens . . . if they had time.

canvas covers for three wagons. Pockets on the inside of each cover held odds and ends, like packets of seeds and sewing needles. Then the canvas was waterproofed with beeswax.

Benjamin Bonney, who was seven, remembered that his father "put in his spare time for months making a strong sturdy wagon in which to cross the plains" to Oregon with the Ides and several other families.

Farmers didn't plow and plant their spring crops because they didn't plan to be around to harvest the wheat or corn. Spring gardens lay untended as wives dried fruit, salted meat, and packed.

Mary Ellen Todd, whose family was emigrating to Oregon, wrote, "As time went on I noticed that father was not taking his customary five or ten minutes just before mealtime for reading his favorite books; and I did not get my lessens quite so regularly, nor commit [memorize] so much of Bobby Burns or other poets."

Instead, her father would say, "Mary Ellen, bring me the saw, or the hammer." Her mother needed her daughter to "help the baby down, or take this little bucket and get some water. . . . Finish this churning while I get my soap to boiling: we'll need a lot of soap you know; also I must finish spinning . . . as we . . . must take with us plenty of yarn."

Young John Roger James hoped they would find lots of fresh meat on the trail to Oregon. He knew that his family had plenty of hardtack, because he had helped make it. Hardtack, dipped in coffee to soften it, wasn't tasty, but it might be the easiest thing to eat on a rainy day.

Father fixed up a place to mix up a lot of dough and knead it with a lever fastened to the wall. He would put a pile of dough into a trough . . . and would have us boys spend the evening kneading the dough thoroughly, then roll it out and cut it into cracker shape about four inches square and then bake them hard and fill them into seamless grain sacks. There would be no lard or butter used, as there would be danger of them spoiling.

John wasn't the only person worrying about food. One emigrant woman noted in her diary two days before starting west that she set up a campfire in front of her house and "was browning coffee and got dinner for the men just to see how it would go."

During the final days, families packed and repacked their belongings. Children brought dolls, slingshots, a pouch of glittering marbles—anything that was special but small. Food staples took up the most space in

A fully loaded wagon should weigh no more than 2,500 pounds, but some families had a hard time leaving anything behind. Later on, travelers discarded chairs, spinning wheels, books, and other heavy items at the side of the trail.

(NATIONAL ARCHIVES)

Preparations and Leaving Home ✦ 17

The day a family left home was sad and heart wrenching, as James F. Wilkins depicted in this 1854 painting.
(Missouri Historical Society)

each wagon. Even so, a few women packed their best dishes in wooden crates filled with sawdust. They crammed trunks with good clothes and a handful of books, such as the family Bible. Farmers packed tools and seeds. Tradesmen brought their tools. Sometimes a loom, a dresser, a gold-framed mirror, or a piano fit inside a wagon, with handmade quilts used as packing material.

The sorting of what to keep and what to leave behind went on to the last day. There wasn't room for everything. Friends and relatives who were staying behind inherited dishes, furniture, and other treasures.

Suddenly, the long winter was over. It was time to head to one of several jumping-off points along the winding Missouri River. For many families, it might take about a month to go three or four hundred miles by wagon from a farm or town to one of the starting points.

Thirteen-year-old Kit, one of six daughters in the large Scott family, wrote her memories of leaving home. Everyone—relatives, elderly grandparents, friends, townspeople, and schoolmates—hugged and cried, knowing they would never see the departing family again. The Scott family had five wagons, painted green and yellow with white canvas covers and filled with food, bedding, clothing, and everything else the family might need. After a quick breakfast on an April morning, the family climbed into the wagons. Kit wrote:

> The word was given, the sluggish oxen started, and the journey of more than two thousand miles was begun . . . of moving wagons, of whips . . . of men walking beside [wagons] with a forced show of indifference, though now and then the back of a brawny hand was drawn hurriedly over the eyes; of silently weeping women and sobbing children, and of an aged grandfather standing at his gate as the wagons filed past, one trembling hand shading his eyes, the other grasping a red handkerchief, his thin gray hair blown back by the fresh breezes, and the soft spring snowflakes falling gently, around him.

Daguerreotypes, like this one taken in 1847, were one of the earliest forms of photography. They were often the only mementos for stay-behind grandparents and other relatives.
(SOUTHERN OREGON HISTORICAL SOCIETY)

Fanny Scott, Kit's nineteen-year-old sister, recalled that "our dog followed us . . . and when Father discovered our dog—Watch—he told him 'Go back home Watch and stay with Grandfather.'" After reaching Oregon, Fanny learned that Watch had returned to the family farm in Illinois and later died.

Another dog, Tiger, from a different family, went west. His thirteen-year-old owner fitted him with leather boots to protect his feet on the journey. Some lucky pets rode most of the way to the West inside a covered wagon.

It was early April in 1846 when the well-to-do Donner and Reed families left Illinois together. The Henderson Party, with Lucy Ann and her brothers and sisters, was ahead of them by a few weeks. Virginia Reed, who was thirteen, wrote: "We were surrounded by loved ones, and there stood all my little schoolmates, who had come to kiss me good-bye. My father with tears in his eyes tried to smile as one friend after another grasped his hands in last farewell. Mama was overcome with grief."

Eliza Donner recalled that "I sat beside my mother with my hand clasped in hers, and we slowly moved away from that quaint old house on its grassy knoll, from the orchard, the corn land, and the meadow. . . . Her clasp tightened, and I glancing up, saw tears in her eyes." Although Eliza was only three at the time, she never forgot that moment.

Fourteen-year-old Sallie Hester, from Bloomington, Indiana, started her diary on March 20, 1849. Just before leaving for California, Sallie wrote that "the last hours were spent in bidding good bye to old friends. My mother is heartbroken over this separation of relatives and friends. The last good bye has been said—the glimpse of our old home, and wave of hand at the old Academy, with a goodbye to kind teachers and schoolmates, and we are off."

Chapter Three

JUMPING OFF

Sixteen-year-old Eliza Ann McAuley left Mt. Pleasant, Iowa, on April 7, 1852, to join her father in California. She traveled with her brother, Tom, who was twenty-two, and her sister, Margaret, who was twenty-eight. Eliza Ann's mother had decided to stay home. Eliza Ann wrote in her little red diary:

> Bade adieu to home and started . . . for the land of gold. Our out-
> fit consists of two light strong wagons drawn by oxen and cows.
> We have two saddle horses and . . . twenty dairy cows, a good sized
> tent and a sheet iron camp stove. . . . We have a plentiful supply of
> dried fruits and vegetables . . . also a quantity of light bread cut in
> slices and dried. Our clothing is light and durable. My sister and I
> wear short dresses and bloomers . . . and a pair of light calf-skin
> topboots for wading through mud and sand.

Eliza Ann McAuley and other emigrants traveled from cities and small farming towns to frontier towns on both sides of the Missouri River. Three-quarters of them came from Indiana, Illinois, Iowa, and Missouri.

April and May were the best times to start. Water was plentiful, and the weather was mild. And, most important, the animals could find the green grass or other feed they needed . . . otherwise they wouldn't have enough energy to pull the wagons. Emigrants had to reach their destinations by September or October, before snows blocked the passes through the mountains.

Before 1849, most families went to Independence, Missouri, which was a starting point for the Santa Fe Trail. It was crowded. Shops had sprung up to supply the emigrants and the Santa Fe traders. There was a constant hammering from a dozen blacksmiths' shops. Oxen and horses were shod; wagons were repaired.

Some came by steamboat up the Missouri River. After 1849, St. Joseph, Missouri, was the main jumping-off point for California's gold rush. With the addition of more steamboats and the building of railroads from the east, other cities farther up the river became popular. By 1852, the Council Bluffs, Iowa–Omaha, Nebraska, area was the number-one departure point for all migrations.

Sallie Hester wrote that her family took the steamboat up the Missouri River to "St. Joe," as she called the city. She was excited because this was her first glimpse "of a river and steamboats . . . and a big city."

What an adventure it must have been for children and young adults! The jumping-off spots were lively places, especially for farm children who were not used to the bustle of city life. Emigrants had been arriving since March, some after wintering in nearby cities. They camped in their tents and wagons near the river. Others found room in town. One man, who was headed to California, reported that he had shared a room with five other men for seventy-five cents.

One of the other starting places for the Santa Fe Trail was Fort Leavenworth in Kansas Territory. Marion Russell and her family planned to take the Santa Fe Trail and go on to California. The Gila

THE SANTA FE TRAIL

At first, the Santa Fe Trail was mainly a trade route. The 775-mile-long road stretched from frontier Missouri southwest across the deserts to Santa Fe in New Mexico Territory.

Spain, then Mexico, controlled Santa Fe and the surrounding areas. The trade route began when Mexico won independence from Spain and opened its doors to business with the United States. William Becknell, one of the first Americans to lead a group of traders to Santa Fe, arrived there in 1821 with pack mules loaded with goods. They sold everything and hurried back home to Missouri with animal furs to sell and leather bags full of silver coins.

Becknell's trip marked the beginning of commercial trade on the Santa Fe Trail. For the next sixty years, mule trains and freight wagon caravans went back and forth on this dusty highway, carrying goods for sale like clothing, cloth, pots and pans, soap, scissors, shovels, axes, and hoes.

After New Mexico became a United States territory in 1846, the trail was also a military route. Army forts were built along the way to protect traders and other travelers from Indian attacks and to provide a supply line for the U.S. Army. Traders and emigrants connected at Santa Fe to take other trails. Both the Gila Trail (going almost due west) and the Old Spanish Trail (going northwest) ended in California. The Mexican Camino Real stretched 1,600 miles from Santa Fe to Mexico City.

By the 1860s, over five thousand wagons a year—traders' caravans, military supply trains, mail wagons, stagecoaches, and settlers' wagons—moved back and forth between the Missouri River area and New Mexico. The Santa Fe Trail faded in importance with the coming of the railroad into the Southwest in the late 1870s.

Trail extension (sometimes called the Southern Emigrant Trail) had been completed in early 1847 by four hundred Mormon soldiers who had been called into service by Brigham Young during the Mexican War. It took the Mormon Battalion four months to widen old pack trails into a military supply and wagon route from Santa Fe to San Diego, California.

People, wagons, and supplies often traveled on major rivers to jumping-off points by steam-powered riverboats. They also used boats like this one near the end of the Oregon Trail, where the Columbia River cuts through the mountains.
(OREGON HISTORICAL SOCIETY)

During the winter of 1851–52, Marion stayed with her widowed mother and her older brother in Kansas City. She went to school, wearing a white pinafore, and listened carefully to the Catholic sisters teach Bible lessons. Marion, who was seven, learned "to make letters on a slate that was bound all around with bright red wool and to rub the letters out with a small yellow sponge that the teacher said had grown down on the bottom of the ocean."

The family moved to nearby Fort Leavenworth in the spring. It was a large, busy military fort. Marion saw "a little city of tents and covered wagons encamped on the edge of the prairies." Traders and soldiers were organizing freight and military wagon trains going west, and Marion's mother hoped to join one.

In the jumping-off towns, young pioneers peeked through wagon flaps at long-haired, buckskin-clad trappers and gold seekers. Everything they saw was new and exciting. Children may have stared at their first western Indians, seemingly naked in breechcloths and moccasins. Some emigrants from the north also saw slaves for the first time. Children were warned that there were thieves among the crowds. On the river, boats hauled freight and people. Steamboat paddles swished, and smokestacks belched out tall plumes of steam.

Jumping-off forts and cities were noisy, busy places. People and creaking wagons pulled in daily. From dawn to dusk, blacksmiths shod animals and forged iron tools. Campfires burned. Corrals of milling stock—beef cattle, milk cows, oxen, mules, and horses—added to the

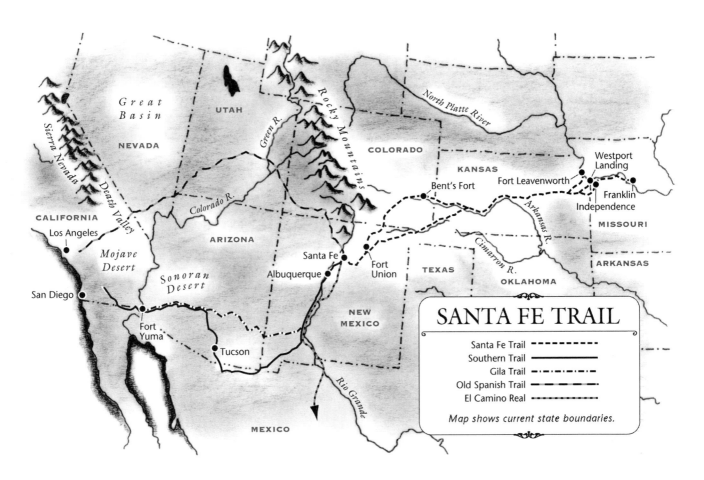

SANTA FE TRAIL

Santa Fe Trail - - - - - - -
Southern Trail ——————
Gila Trail -·-·-·-·-·-
Old Spanish Trail —·—·—·—
El Camino Real ·············

Map shows current state boundaries.

noises, smells, and dust. The sound of gunshots, as men and boys tested out the latest "shooting iron," filled the air. Evenings, someone might strum a banjo or work a harmonica. Gamblers, with hidden derringers, organized card games. In all this confusion, emigrants still found time to write a letter home or jot a sentence or two in a journal.

Sallie Hester wrote that her family was "laying in supplies for the trip. . . . As far as the eye can reach, so great is the emigration, you see nothing but wagons . . . a vast army on wheels—crowds of men, women, and lots of children."

The Reed and Donner families arrived at their jumping-off point, Independence, Missouri, together. Eliza Donner's father was a farmer, like many of the men who went west. The rest of the men were mostly blacksmiths, carpenters, teachers, doctors, editors, and preachers. Other families met one another for the first time at the jumping-off point and formed a wagon train then. A lone traveler might sign up, too.

It was a time of waiting and work. If the roads were too muddy, the

These emigrant wagons stop at Manhattan, Kansas, to purchase supplies in 1860.
(KANSAS STATE HISTORICAL SOCIETY)

heavy wagons would sink. Boys helped their fathers stow extra wagon parts under wagon beds. They sharpened tools and greased the wooden axles on which the wheels turned. At stores sometimes called the "Last Chance," travelers bought tools, ropes, water buckets, clothing, harnesses, and other supplies, like knives, rifles, powder, lead, and shot. And everything cost three or four times as much as at home.

The men and their sons talked to old mountain men and others who knew the West. They asked all kinds of questions. How wide and deep were the rivers? Were there places to ford them? What about snow? When did it fall in the western mountains? And desert crossings? Where were the passes in the mountains? What should they expect from Indians?

Joined by their daughters, women chatted with one another about supplies, making sure they had enough of everything. They organized their "grub boxes," which were at the end or side of each wagon. Helen Carpenter, a young bride of nineteen from Kansas, wrote that she packed "a Dutch oven, a camp kettle, frying pan, and coffee pot—these with some tin plates, cups, tin spoons, knives and forks; a rolling-pin, bread pan, milk can and a smoothing iron."

Some emigrants wanted to travel alone. Moses Laird was only seventeen when he left Ohio, hoping to get to either California or Oregon. He recalled that he "got 2 carpet sacks and packed up my tools, some [clothes], with a large oil cloth coat to protect me from the storms on the plains, and . . . with forty five Dollars in my pockets . . . I shouldered my carpet sacks and started alone." He may have eventually joined a wagon train for safety.

Martin's Groceries in St. Joseph, Missouri, placed this 1853 newspaper ad in hopes of selling provisions to pioneers leaving for California.
(STATE HISTORICAL SOCIETY OF MISSOURI)

Families often hired unmarried men to help with the work. John Minto left his coal-mining parents and siblings in Pittsburgh, Pennsylvania, to find adventure by going west. His Oregon-bound employer promised that John would have

> bed and board, and have your washing and mending done, and you shall give me your help as I require, to get my family and effects to Oregon. I have four guns, and two wagons, and . . . my oldest children will be able to keep up the loose stock; so that one of us can be spared to hunt every day if we choose, and you shall have your turn at that.

These children and their pet dog posed for a picture before they traveled on the Mormon Trail in the 1860s.

The hired men soon became trusted family members. Midway into his 1844 trip, John Minto wrote that "the old and the young of the family seemed already something like father and mother and brothers and sisters to me . . . our traveling family of ten."

Edwin Pettit, an orphan, was only thirteen when he snuck out of the house one night in Nauvoo, Illinois. He tiptoed past his sleeping guardian, carrying his shoes. "Disguised as a girl, and in company with four or five girls, I crossed the Des Moines river on a flat boat. . . . I was wearing a wig and sidecombs in my hair, and also wearing a sunbonnet." On the opposite bank of the river, a friend met Edwin with a horse. "As is well known, girls are supposed to ride sidewise, I also took that precaution." Edwin joined his sister and her husband, who were going to Utah.

In each newly formed wagon train, the men and older boys, like Edwin, helped elect a captain, or wagon train master, as he was also called. They voted on trail rules.

Edward Lenox's father was captain of their wagon train in 1843. It wasn't an easy job, recalled Samuel Tetherow, whose father led a train from Missouri to Oregon two years later. "My dad was a pretty good man. He was capable as well as popular. . . . But if you think it's any snap to run a wagon train of 66 wagons with every man in the train having a different idea of what is the best thing to do, all I can say is that some day you ought to try it."

The decisions a captain made were the law. Each captain had to decide which route to take, when to rest, when to leave, where to stop, for how long, who stood guard, and whether or not the wagon train would move on Sunday. The captain picked each campsite, taking into consideration the amount of wood, water, and grass available. He might also decide to exclude families who had slaves. Many migrating families did not want to worry about the slavery issue in their new western home.

Wagon trains hired scouts to lead them west. They were paid any-

SETH KINMAN,

California Hunter and Trapper, who presented President Lincoln with the Elk Horn Chair.

Entered according to Act of Congress by Seth Kinman, in the year 1864, in the Clerk's office of the District Court for the District of Columbia.

Brady   *Washington.*

Mountain men like Seth Kinman, who knew the trails and understood the different Indian tribes, were often hired as guides.
(THE HUNTINGTON LIBRARY)

where from one to four dollars a day. Sarah Ide recalled that "our [scout's] name was 'Old Greenwood.' [He and his two half-Crow Indian sons] were mountain men and dressed the same as Indians. . . . I was more afraid of these . . . men than of the wild Indians."

Spring arrived, with rains that washed away the snow. The sun began to dry out the muddy roads. Children and parents hoped they were ready for the four- to six-month-long trip. Whether they were or not, it was time to leave the jumping-off points and go west!

Chapter Four

HOPING TO GO TWENTY MILES IN A DAY

In the early days along the trail, there were no bridges over any streams or rivers. To cross the Missouri River, wagons were rolled onto flatboats made of logs and powered by huge oars. An oarsman stood up and used both arms to control the oars. Everyone and everything might get soaked. The Missouri was only the first of many river and stream crossings during the journey.

Explorer Meriwether Lewis, in a letter home to his mother about the Missouri, had warned future travelers of "the rapidity of it's current, it's falling banks, sandbars, and timber . . . in the water . . . with large masses of earth about their roots . . . drifting with the stream."

Nearly fifty years after Lewis's trip, Eliza Ann McAuley wrote:

> **Monday, May 10th.** There are thousands of wagons waiting to be ferried over.

> **Tuesday, May 11th.** Got up early and took the wagons down a little nearer the ferry, so as to take advantage of the first opportunity to cross.

Wednesday, May 12th. Wind blew furiously today and the ferry could do very little business.

Saturday, May 15th. Got . . . one of our wagons [across this morning], leaving the rest of our train on the eastern side.

Sunday, May 16th. This morning was very cold and disagreeable, the wind blowing a perfect gale and the sand flying in clouds. . . . The boys . . . have been ferrying all day, bringing the rest of our train across this evening.

Nine-year-old Catherine Sager wrote about crossing the Missouri on a ferry with her family's wagon. She and her brothers and sisters began to cry in fear of the river "that came rushing down and seemed as though it would swallow [us] up."

Sarah Ide rode her horse sidesaddle and, with her father and the hired help, coaxed 28 oxen and 165 cattle into the Missouri River. Men and teenage boys prodded the rest of the animals until they swam across the river. Then they gathered up the scattered stock on the other side.

Eliza Ann McAuley and other emigrants often had to wait for days for their turn to cross the wide, muddy Missouri River by ferry, as depicted in this painting by William Henry Jackson.
(SCOTTS BLUFF NATIONAL MONUMENT)

Thomas Chambers, who was twenty when his family started for Oregon, wrote about the "first, last and only time I cried while crossing the plains." He lost some of his family's flour when his raft overturned. "I thought the family would starve."

In May and part of June, most emigrants followed a trail over the grass-covered lands. Everyone followed the same ruts, and it was easy going. On a good day of twelve hours of travel, they went about fifteen to twenty miles. The pioneers knew it would not be so easy in the desert and mountains.

During this part of the trip, large wagon companies might divide and then divide again. It was hard to make headway in big groups. One train going west in 1845 had 480 wagons. Eventually they broke into groups of about twenty each.

Besides rivers, there were dozens of creeks and damp streambeds to ford. No one wanted a wagon to get stuck in the mud or break an axle. Sometimes the pioneers cut trees and brush to throw into the streams or muddy ravines so that animals and wagons could pass over them. This might take three or four hours . . . or longer.

Children were happy to be away from school. They didn't have to memorize poetry, study spelling, or do math. Annie Cannon, age fourteen, would rather drive the wagon or spend time with her brother, George, even though he reminded her to get her books from the wagon and do her lessons. Later, after she settled in Utah, she reflected that "I missed the best opportunity I ever had. I have been very sorry."

Books like the McGuffey's *Readers,* Webster's *Spelling Book,* or Frost's *Pictorial History of the United States* were tucked away in trunks. No one was too interested in studying. "The first part of [the route] is beautiful and the scenery surpassing anything of the kind I have ever seen—large rolling prairies stretching as far as your eye can carry you," wrote twelve-year-old Elizabeth Keegan in a letter home to Missouri in 1852. "The grass so green and flowers of every description

Magazines printed frequent stories and illustrations of trail life. This illustration is from a Harper's Monthly *1874 cover.*

from violets to geraniums of the richest hue." As one fourteen-year-old recalled, "We looked upon [the trip] . . . as a great picnic." And in the beginning, he was correct.

Helen Carpenter, who was also going to California, agreed with Elizabeth Keegan and wrote on May 27, 1857, that "this is certainly the most beautiful country. The grass is from one to 10 feet high, and there is a profusion of wild flowers all over the prairie. But . . . the rattlesnakes are as thick as the leaves on the trees . . . and I can bid

Kansas Good Bye without regret." Throughout her journal, Helen continued to write strongly about the things she liked and didn't like about the trip.

Beyond the Missouri Valley, the tall grasses changed to tightly sodded grass. The pioneers followed the ridges, nervously looking for Indians, even though the tribes in eastern Kansas were friendly. In many places, narrow buffalo trails crisscrossed the land.

Emigrants woke before sunrise. Mothers and daughters cooked on a stove made of thin sheets of iron or tin. As wood became less available on the prairie, the metal stoves were left beside the trail. Women switched to an open fire or a trench on the windy prairie. They cooked with dried buffalo chips, grass, or brush—whatever they and their children could find. It was a daily battle to keep the burning embers from scorching their skirts and aprons.

Pioneers cooked meals over an open fire with a cast-iron kettle, spider, and coffeepot. Sketch by J. G. Bruff.
(THE HUNTINGTON LIBRARY)

Food simmered in a cast-iron kettle or a spider—an iron pot with three legs long enough to straddle the flames. Charles Young, who was heading to Colorado's gold fields in 1865, learned to make skillet bread, as did many earlier travelers. He stirred together flour and salt, probably with bacon fat, and added saleratus (called baking soda today) to make the bread rise. Some cooks had eggs, butter, or buttermilk to add, but not Charles.

After the coals were ready, Charles spread them out evenly and placed the skillet on them. "A chunk [of dough] was cut off and put in the skillet, the lid placed and covered with coals; in fifteen minutes we would have as nice a looking loaf of bread as one could wish to see. . . . When eaten warm, it was very palatable, but when cold, only bull whackers could digest it."

STEADY OR STUBBORN?

It was critical to pick the best animals. They would have to pull a heavy wagon for two thousand miles or more. Should they be mules or oxen?

Mules ate grain, which had to be stored in the wagon, taking up valuable storage space. But mules walked faster than oxen. Pioneers who used mules often reached the end of the trail more quickly, cutting their travel time by about a week or two. Mules were more surefooted than oxen on the rockier parts of the trail. Yet, as many muleskinners learned, these stubborn, unpredictable animals could kick viciously with their hind legs or spook and run at the sight of their own shadow.

Slower-moving oxen walked twelve to fifteen miles a day and ate almost anything, even sagebrush. They were harnessed in pairs with wooden yokes, and the yokes were not removed when the animals grazed. But oxen tended to go lame on the rocky or cactus-filled parts of the trail. If that happened, the oxen were killed.

A pair of oxen cost between $40 and $160, much less than two mules. It was for this reason that most pioneers picked oxen.

One bride almost gave up on the first windy day. Three experienced trail men came to her rescue. One man held his hat over the fire; another held his over the coffeepot, and a third man set his hat over a frying pan of sizzling bacon. Somehow sand still swirled into the coffeepot. That day, the young cook learned a valuable trick—to strain "the coffee through an old dish rag" before serving it to her husband.

The men and boys in the wagon train harnessed the oxen to the wagons and saddled the horses. Following breakfast, women and children loaded the wagons with the tents, blankets, and pots and pans. By seven o'clock in the morning, everyone was ready. Harnesses jangled and hundreds of hooves pounded the ground as each wagon fell into place. In the large trains, wagons, animals, and people stretched for as long as a mile over the prairie. White canvas tops billowed and snapped like sheets drying in the wind.

The wagon train stopped for an hour or two at noon. Families might spread out a waterproof sheet and sit on it or use boxes for chairs. Marion Russell, whose mother found a job as a cook for a military train going to Santa Fe, recalled eating cold lunches, like leftover biscuits dipped in molasses. They ate with tin plates and cups that would not break.

Then everyone rested. Marion crawled to the back of the wagon to play with her doll or sleep on a pile of blankets. "I can [still] see the tired sweaty mules rolling over and over in the grass delighted to be free of the heavy wagons. I can see the tired drivers . . . lying under the shade of the wagons, their hats covering their faces as they slept."

After the nooning, the train went on. Will, Marion's older brother, walked with the driver next to the mules. Marion sat on the board seat at the front of the wagon beside her mother. She learned how to jump off the lumbering wagon as it rolled slowly onward. Except for the sick, the babies, and a few pioneers who rode saddle horses, everyone walked all or part of the day. There just wasn't room in the crowded wagons for the entire family, and they added too much weight for the animals to pull easily.

Six-year-old Billy Walker told an adult, "I'm a great hand for walking: I walked all day yesterday, last night; and when we camped here, on the hill, I said I wasn't tired, and I wasn't."

Each night, the captain, with the help of his scout, found a place to stop. The wagons formed a corral to protect the group from Indians and wild animals. The tongue of one wagon was chained to the rear wheel of its neighbor to form a fence, usually in a circle or oblong shape.

It was a lively scene, with pitched tents of every size, shape, and color. There were campfires, animals, and people busy at work. Rifles, saddles, harnesses, trunks, and all kinds of other gear lay on the ground. People were talking, singing, laughing, and whistling. A few might be arguing or even cursing their oxen as they checked on them one last time.

To the sound of a harmonica or fiddle, and families chatting around the campfire, emigrants began to settle for the night. Women and children slept inside the wagons or in tents. The men and drivers bedded down under the wagons or near the still-warm campfire. On cold nights, a buffalo robe or blanket covered the snoring traveler.

Mary Burrell, a teenager from Illinois, wrote, "Always sleep sound no matter how much noise is going on."

During the early weeks, the weather was generally good. It gave the

Sometimes canvas was stretched between two wagons to create a sleeping area. Henry Smith and his seven children posed in camp before going on to Colorado.
(DENVER PUBLIC LIBRARY, WESTERN HISTORY COLLECTION)

greenhorns—shopkeepers, doctors, and other nonfarmers who didn't have much experience with mules or oxen—time to learn how to handle them. Frisky young animals that had been bought at the jumping-off spots began to settle into the daily job of pulling wagons.

Catherine Sager, her parents, and her two brothers and three sisters left for Oregon in 1844. Catherine remembered that "Father's outfit consisted of one large wagon; to this he had two yoke of well-broken oxen; the rest were young and unbroken, and as he was not used to driving he had much difficulty." The captain had to teach Catherine's father how to control the team of oxen.

Many trains stopped on Sundays and held religious services. Most of the travelers were devout churchgoers. Some were against dancing, card playing, or drinking alcohol. One boy wrote that his parents believed that the fiddle was an invention of the devil to lure people to hell. Fifteen-year-old Mary Eliza Warner from Illinois wrote: "Aunt Celia and I played Chess which [our neighbor] thought was the first step toward gambling."

Two to three months into the trip, some wagon trains were already behind schedule and had to travel seven days a week in order to get over the mountains before winter. For many women and children, this was a moral problem, and they were upset that they could not "keep the Lord's Day holy" by resting and worshiping on Sundays.

Rachel Taylor was part of what was called the "preachers' wagon train" because there were three Methodist ministers among the group going to southern Oregon. Rachel, who was fifteen, wrote on June 19, 1853, that "the men took two tents and put them together in such a way as to make a large awning and quite an audience gathered under it to hear preaching. Several companies . . . camped at a short distance from here, and all came out to meeting."

Sundays were also a day of rest for the animals. In addition to the oxen teams, families usually brought milk cows and several saddle horses. Large herds grazed two or three miles away from camp and

During stops, emigrants caught up on chores, like washing clothes and spreading them out to dry. Perhaps these travelers' mules or oxen were grazing nearby.

(MUSEUM OF NEW MEXICO/BEN WITTICK)

were guarded by several men or young boys. As one traveler said, "Our lives depend on our animals."

Boys helped their fathers mend harnesses and wagon parts. To keep the wooden wheels from drying out too much, they greased them with boot leather oil, soap, and even bacon fat. The men painted gutta-percha, a kind of rubber, on the canvas covers to keep them water-proof. They checked the wooden parts for damage, including the hickory bows that held the canvas's shape. It was also important to clean their guns. They might not fire properly if they were damp or starting to rust inside.

After a rainstorm, women dried out the bedding, boxes, and barrels. Each woman opened her flour, coffee, sugar, and salt containers to the dry air. Children helped their mothers sort the moldy rice, beans, corn-meal, and dried fruit from the fresh.

Eighteen-year-old Eugenia Zieber, who was going to Oregon, kept a diary during her trip. She remembered one particular Sunday when the wagon train camped next to a river. "We have a most lovely place to wash. Good water for washing close at hand, we are shaded by trees, and there are bushes near by on which we can spread the clothes. The water looks tempting. How pleasant it would be to go in wading."

Another young pioneer, Lucy, did go in. "Ma and I just have been to bathe in the Sweetwater [River], but, oh, it was cold! We could only take two or three dips and then run out."

Clothes dried in the sun, but if the wagon train moved on too soon, a mother wrote that "we wore them just as they dried. We were not particular about our looks." Many pioneers had packed trunks of clothing, but within a few short weeks, they discovered that it was simpler to slip on the same outfit each day, even if it was dirty.

Back home, women and girls had dressed in floor-length dresses, with petticoats under their skirts. For women and teenage girls, having narrow waists was fashionable, even if it meant wearing a tight corset. On the frontier and going west, they wore simple cotton calico dresses. It was hard to keep the long skirts out of the dust and mud. Bonnets helped to protect them from the sun.

Eliza Ann McAuley and a few other young women switched to bloomer outfits—shorter skirts over pants that reached their shoe tops. It was a radical style in those days, and women or girls who wore them were occasionally accused of looking and acting like men. Although the bloomer outfits were popular with some women on the trail, many thought that the outfits were too extreme.

Most men and boys still wore pants and cotton or flannel shirts, but some adopted the style of the mountain men and dressed in animal skins.

Children walked barefoot, and their feet grew tough. Later, when

Amelia Bloomer invented a combination skirt and pants outfit in 1851.
(AUTHOR'S COLLECTION)

These pioneers are enjoying green grass, rolling hills, and good weather.
(MUSEUM OF NEW MEXICO/J. CARBUTT)

the ground turned rocky, they would wear homemade shoes of leather. There were no right or left shoes at the time. A pair was put on, soaked in water, and allowed to dry on the wearer's feet. Younger children might inherit an outgrown pair of shoes from an older brother or sister. Or they traded for moccasins with the Indians.

Six or even seven days a week, the wagon trains headed west. Many journal writers noted that the scenery was boring in the beginning, with the never-changing open space and tall grass. It was easy travel at first. But farther into the trip, unpredictable events seemed to break up the daily routine. As Rachel Taylor wrote on the way to Oregon, "We were delayed in the morning as a new ox yoke had to be constructed to take the place of the broken one." And two weeks later, she noted that the train "did not start until late as the broken wagon had to be repaired."

In another diary entry, Eugenia Zieber wrote that "[we] camped out and slept in our tent. . . . We have had very pleasant weather generally, and are all in good spirits enjoying ourselves." Eugenia was writing about her parents, as well as her three younger sisters and a little brother. A few weeks into the trip, they had to stop unexpectedly because, as they crossed a ditch, a chain connecting the horses broke. Much to their surprise, it was snowing and "the wind was blowing hard" as they pulled the wagon from the ditch, repaired the chain, and hitched up the horses again.

The next day, the family started early. The weather was fine, and Eugenia reported that they sat on a log and ate supper with "trees looking fresh & happy around you and flowers peeping up from the bright grass."

After supper, it usually took travelers a while to settle down for the night. In the big wagon trains, it was especially hard to keep all the animals in one place, even with guards watching over them. A few might wander off in search of better grass or fresh water. Or a sudden thunderstorm could cause them to stampede and run for miles. The men and boys could use up half a day or longer to find them again.

Although wagon trains hoped to go about fifteen to twenty miles a day, this seldom happened. Lost animals or children, mud, time-consuming river crossings, childbirth, and numerous other events caused delays. Some days, they never moved at all.

Chapter Five

OREGON OR BUST

Edward Lenox and his father, who lived in Missouri, heard a speaker brag about the many wonders of Oregon in the spring of 1843. "They do say that out in Oregon, the pigs are running about under the great acorn trees, round and fat, and already cooked, with knives and forks sticking in them so that you can cut off a slice whenever you are hungry." A few months later, the Lenox family, with a covered wagon pulled by a team of oxen, was waiting to cross the Missouri River.

"My father was one of the restless ones who are not content to remain in one place long at a time," Catherine Sager wrote in her memoirs. Her father had listened to another speaker, Dr. Marcus Whitman, who ran a mission in Oregon Country. The Whitman Mission was already a popular stopping spot on the trail. It was expanding every year, with gardens, ponds, and orchards, plus a blacksmith shop, grist mill, and house. The Sagers joined a wagon train called the "Independence Colony," and many of the canvas covers bore messages like "Oregon or Bust."

Other families were swayed by John Charles Frémont, a soldier and explorer. Guided by Kit Carson, Frémont surveyed the Oregon Trail to South Pass for the United States government. Families read the detailed reports of his many explorations. The maps and reports published by "The Pathfinder," as Frémont was called, were also read by some Mormons and helped convince them to travel to the Great Salt Lake Valley.

Land-hungry settlers first used the Oregon Trail in 1841. Emigrants picked Oregon for many reasons: for the balmy climate, for the rich soil in the wide Willamette Valley, for adventure, and to attempt to outnumber the British settlers on land that they believed didn't belong to the British. After the Oregon Treaty of 1846, the land became part of the United States.

The route started at any one of the jumping-off cities along the

A Mormon family rests in front of its wagons in 1867.

OREGON-CALIFORNIA TRAIL

Oregon Trail - - - - - - -
California Trail · · · · · · ·
Oregon-California Trail ——————

Map shows current state boundaries.

Missouri River and ended in Oregon's Willamette Valley. In between, there were prairies and mountains to cross, deserts, and then more mountains. Travelers did not look forward to the miles of intense heat, lack of water, sand, or snow, but instead dreamed about the promise of a better life in Oregon and other places. They were not scared off by people like Daniel Webster, who wrote that the Far West was a "region of savages and wild beasts."

Once the emigrants reached the far side of the Missouri River, recalled ten-year-old Mary Ackley, "we were outside the pale of civil law. We were in Indian country, where no civilized government existed." For Mary and others, the main part of the trip was really under way. Weeks later, and some 460 miles west of the Missouri River, emigrants reached a place where the Platte River's north and south forks flow together.

After crossing the South Platte, the scenery changed. Wagon trains went up, across, then down a dry, tablelike plateau, then followed the sandy banks of the North Platte River. Various earth and rock formations—Courthouse, Chimney Rock, and others—intrigued the travelers. For seven-year-old Jesse Applegate, who was part of an 1843 expedition to Oregon, Chimney Rock seemed "to touch the sky."

The wagon trains passed a large clay-and-sandstone formation known as Scotts Bluff and reached Fort Laramie a few days later. In the early years, this fort was the last American outpost of importance. Sallie Hester, who was going west with her parents, wrote:

> This fort is of adobe, enclosed with a high wall of the same. The entrance is a hole in the wall just large enough for a person to crawl through. The impression you have on entering is that you are in a small town. We stayed here some time looking at everything that was to be seen and enjoying it to the fullest extent after our long tramp. We camped one mile from the fort, where we remained a few days to wash and lighten up.

Yoked pairs of animals, oxen or mules, usually pulled each wagon. It wasn't always easy going.
(Denver Public Library, Western History Collection)

FORT LARAMIE

Fort Laramie was built near the fur trappers' trail on the Laramie River, close to where it joins the Platte River in what is now the state of Wyoming. It is about one-third of the way west from jumping-off places along the Missouri River.

The Cheyenne, Sioux, and Arapaho hunted buffalo on the plains and sold the hides at the fort. Fort Laramie hosted trappers and missionaries, plus the first emigrants who came in 1841, on the Oregon Trail. It soon became a well-known stopping point and supply center for western travel.

Following the gold rush in California, large emigrant camps often spread out beyond the fort. Travelers bought fresh draft animals, flour, and medicines, and they repaired worn equipment before crossing the Rocky Mountains. They also traded with the Plains Indian tribes.

Tensions grew between the two groups as more and more emigrants passed over the Indians' hunting grounds. The U.S. Army bought Fort Laramie in 1849 and made it into a major military post. More and more soldiers came to protect the emigrants at the fort and along the trail. Eventually, the United States government forced the Indians onto reservations, and in 1890, Fort Laramie was closed.

The U.S. Army's Fort Laramie was an important resupply point for wagon trains. Prior to 1849, when the fort was privately owned, it was called Fort William and then Fort John.
(State Historical Society of Wisconsin/James F. Wilkins)

Most Oregon-bound wagon trains hoped to reach Independence Rock in present-day Wyoming by the middle of July. Whenever possible, they followed the Sweetwater River. Jesse Applegate was disappointed that the water tasted bitter. He wondered if the Green River, ahead on the route, would really be green.

Pioneers camped near Independence Rock, and before moving on, they wrote or carved their names on this landmark. When Helen Carpenter explored the large, loaf-shaped rock, she wrote: "Saw several names high up on the sides and placed mine there writing it with tar."

Elisha Brooks added his name. Charley True, who had come from Minnesota, didn't, but he noted that "there were hundreds and hundreds of names done in lamp-black and oil, axle grease, paint—anything that could be daubed on. . . . It was here we found the names of J. C. Fremont, Brigham Young, Kit Carson and many other[s]."

Beyond Independence Rock, pioneers passed Devil's Gate, another famous landmark. The trail was rough. They began the slow ascent of the Rocky Mountains through barren land dotted with sagebrush and greasewood.

This stretch of the trip tested the tempers of men and the energies of the animals, Sarah Cummins recalled. It had been months since her family had left Missouri. Whips cracked and language turned colorful. Sarah said that her "dear mother would almost invariably say, 'You go on ahead,'" and she would ride out of earshot on her horse.

Later in July or early August, they reached a wide-open valley in the Rocky Mountains called South Pass. It crested on the Continental Divide, seven thousand feet above sea level. The ascent was so gradual that some pioneers didn't even realize that they had reached the backbone of the Rocky Mountains.

South Pass was a familiar spot to the old mountain men who were now guiding the wagon trains. Ahead of the travelers, the creeks and rivers flowed toward Oregon and the Pacific Ocean, and behind them

Independence Rock, along the Sweetwater River, was the halfway point on the Oregon Trail. The notch in the distance is Devil's Gate. Painting by William Henry Jackson.
(UTAH STATE HISTORICAL SOCIETY)

all the waters flowed eastward, in the direction of their former homes.

The mountain air was cold, and the peaks gleamed white with snow. At the high altitude, snow might fall during the summer. A young pioneer wrote that she "gathered snow for a snowballing." The ground could freeze overnight. One man who slept outside discovered on waking up that his hair "being very long, the ends were froze to the . . . ground, so that I had to pull it loose, but had to leave some . . . for the wolves to examine."

It was hard going in what is present-day Idaho. Travelers splashed through creeks and followed faint Indian and animal trails along the Snake River. The climb over the Blue Mountains in what is now eastern Oregon was also difficult. Everyone was tired, and the animals were weak from the long journey. The forest was damp and cold, especially at night.

Jesse Applegate remembered that "the trees were cut just near to the ground to allow the wagons to pass over the stumps, and the road through the forest was only cleared out wide enough for a wagon to pass along."

In the early years, there was no road over the Cascade Mountains to the west. Using the tools they brought with them, emigrants built large wooden boats or log rafts near the Columbia River at The Dalles, which means "rapids" in French and was named by early French travelers for the many rapids at the site. Sometimes they left their wagons behind or took the wheels off and set the wagon bed on the raft. The animals were sold at Fort Walla Walla. The pioneers planned to purchase fresh animals at Fort Vancouver, after the water part of their journey. Jesse wrote that "the faithful oxen, now sore-necked [and] sore-footed, had marched week after week, and month after month, drawing those wagons with their loads from the Missouri River to the Columbia . . . and were unhitched for the last time."

It was a scary trip down the Columbia River. Boats had to go over rapid after rapid. The Applegate family used two boats. Jesse recalled going around a bend in the river and seeing rapids ahead. "There was a wail of anguish, a shriek, and a scene of confusion. . . . The boat we were watching disappeared and we saw the men and boys struggling in the water." Warren, Jesse's older brother, was never seen again.

Another Oregon-bound traveler filled the bed of a covered wagon with soil and planted apple, pear, plum, and cherry trees. The trees were three to five feet high. Everyone teased the farmer, but he got his young orchard across the plains. After wrapping the trees and roots carefully, the pioneer and his nursery floated down the Columbia River. Many of those trees were the parent stock for today's orchards in the Willamette Valley.

The Barlow Road over the mountains was completed in 1846, and settlers no longer needed to risk life-threatening river travel. But there were still creeks and smaller rivers to ford. They were hard on wagons and people. Sarah Cummins helped by riding her horse ahead. "In case

a stream was very treacherous, as to hidden rocks, I would ride in front and discover hidden boulders."

The Oregon Trail ended in Oregon City. Some pioneers, like the Applegate family, veered south to settle in the Willamette River valley area and think about farming once again.

About eleven thousand people had settled in Oregon by 1848; most were farming families from the Midwest. The fertile Willamette Valley south of Oregon City began to flourish. Starting in 1850, the United States government granted each unmarried man 320 acres. The amount was doubled for married men. Twelve years later, there were over fifty thousand settlers in Oregon, lured by the promise of good farmland.

Chapter Six

CALIFORNIA GOLD

AND OTHER DESTINATIONS

In 1844 Elisha Stevens led the first emigrant wagon train to California by way of Council Bluffs, Iowa. Other trains followed. Along the trail, there were always uncertainties about the route. The men argued about whether or not to take shortcuts. Lucy Ann Henderson was eleven when she and her family traveled west in 1846:

> You have no idea of the confusion and uncertainty in the minds of the emigrants as to which was the best route to take. [Some] had started out with the intention of going to California, while others, meeting California boosters at Fort Laramie or Fort Bridger [a small trading post], changed their original plans and took the California Trail in place of going on to the Willamette Valley [in Oregon].
>
> Some said you had to buy the land in California, while in Oregon it was free. Others said Oregon had the best climate, but it was much easier to go to California. Some advised us to take the short cuts across the 45-mile desert, avoiding going to Fort Bridger.

✦ ✦ ✦

John Sutter, who owned a fort near Sacramento, California, wanted settlers. He had lots of land that the Mexican government had given him. He sent mountain man Caleb Greenwood and his sons to Fort Hall in Idaho to convince emigrants to come to California instead of Oregon.

Benjamin Bonney and his family were headed to Oregon in 1845. So were Sarah Ide and her family. Benjamin recalled meeting Greenwood at Fort Hall. "[He] was dressed in buckskins and had a long heavy beard and used very picturesque language. He said the road was dangerous on account of the Indians. . . . To California there was an easy grade and crossing the mountains would not be difficult."

Caleb Greenwood was a good speaker. He told the travelers that Sutter would give them potatoes, coffee, sugar, and meat once they reached California. Sutter also promised every man some of his Mexican land grant.

The next morning, Benjamin recalled, "old Caleb Greenwood said that all you who want to go to California . . . follow me." Eight wagons, including those belonging to the Ides and Bonneys, left the train. They paid Greenwood $125, which was good pay in 1845, to guide them to California.

The rest of the pioneers started for Oregon, shouting, "Good-bye, we will never see you again. Your bones will whiten in the desert or be gnawed by the wild animals in the mountains."

Benjamin Bonney's group reached the desert two weeks later. After crossing it, they started up the eastern side of the Sierra Nevada. It took them four hard days to reach the summit, Benjamin recalled. The small wagon train "camped by a beautiful, ice-cold, crystal-clear mountain stream. We camped there for three days to rest the teams and let the women wash the clothing and get things fixed up."

It was October when they reached the edge of the Sacramento Valley. At Sutter's Fort, Benjamin and his family were welcomed. They had

housing, food, and work, but no land. The following spring, in 1846, the Bonneys moved to Oregon because the Mexican government wanted them to give up their United States citizenship.

The Bonneys should have stayed in California a little bit longer. The United States acquired California and other western lands on February 2, 1848, when a treaty was signed in Mexico following the Mexican War of 1846–1848. At that time, news between the East Coast and the West Coast traveled slowly. Not many people knew what had happened several days earlier, on January 24, 1848, in California.

James W. Marshall, a carpenter, had been inspecting a sawmill he and his crew were building for John Sutter about forty-five miles up the American River from Sutter's Fort. Marshall had come to Oregon with the Sager wagon train in 1844 but later moved to California.

That day in January 1848, Marshall spotted some small flakes of shining yellow metal on the river bottom. He picked them up. Some were tiny; others were bigger than a kernel of wheat. "Hey, boys," he called out, "I believe I've found a gold mine."

Pioneers stocked up on supplies and rested at Fort Hall before going on to either Oregon or California. Sketch by J. G. Bruff.
(THE HUNTINGTON LIBRARY)

James Marshall, in front of Sutter's Mill on the American River, where he discovered gold in 1848.

Within weeks, word of Marshall's find spread. By May, San Francisco had caught gold fever. "The blacksmith dropped his hammer, the farmer his sickle, the baker his loaf. . . . I have only women left . . . and a gang of prisoners," an official in one town wrote. San Francisco and other California cities practically closed down.

As word fanned out, Americans who lived east of the Mississippi River decided to go overland to California in the spring of 1849 to find their "pot of gold." They called themselves forty-niners.

The discovery of gold in California in 1848 transformed the migration into a stampede. The next year nearly ninety thousand gold seekers, mostly men, swarmed to California by sea, through Mexico, or directly across the United States. About fifteen hundred children and teenagers, traveling with their families, reached the diggings by covered wagon.

One man watched 5,516 wagons roll by Fort Kearny during the spring of 1849. He estimated that there were twenty thousand people on the road, and more coming. During the rest of his trip to California, he passed a thousand abandoned wagons.

In one three-mile stretch, another pioneer counted five hundred dead oxen. Some men, he believed, were so eager to get to the gold fields that they lost all sense of right or wrong and pushed their oxen to their deaths. Trunks, clothing, shoes, and even food were cast aside. Owners who could not use these goods often destroyed them by pouring turpentine on food or burning wagons and clothes. They were determined that no one else would benefit.

More than fifty thousand people may have been on the Oregon-California Trail in 1850, the peak year, and they traveled by wagon, on horseback, and even on foot. The ground was worn bare by people, wheels, and animals. Not a blade of grass could grow.

"The further west I proceeded, the more intense became the California fever," wrote a journalist who was going west. Train leaders

Humorous ads encouraged thousands of people to take ships around the tip of South America to California rather than travel overland.
(MUSEUM OF THE CITY OF NEW YORK)

talked about taking cutoffs to speed up the trip. Small groups of wagons left their wagon trains to push ahead more quickly. As one fourteen-year-old recalled, "They were anxious to hurry on without the Sunday stops."

Over the years of migration, there were several "parting of the ways." The Sublette Cutoff, between South Pass and Fort Hall, was popular during California's

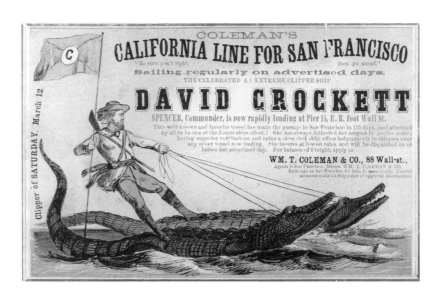

These miners are using a high-pressure water system to wash gold from the rocky hillside. This photograph is unusual in the number of women and girls pictured—men outnumbered women twenty to one in the early years of the gold rush.

gold rush because it could save five or six days of travel. But the fifty-mile-long route had no trees, grass, or drinkable water.

For California-bound travelers, the desert section came when supplies were low, animals were weak, and the wagons were in poor condition. The final challenge was to get over the Sierra Nevada before the first snowfall.

Elizabeth Keegan wrote: "After you cross the last of the mountains you descend into the Sacramento valley long looked for by the weary emigrant. The heat can scarcely be endured, particularly so on first coming down from the mountains."

California grew from 14,000 people to 115,000 people in 1849. A year later, California became a state. By then, the main trails were well marked. Guidebooks, like Joseph Ware's *The Emigrant's Guide to*

San Francisco before and after the discovery of gold, as drawn in 1850. (AUTHOR'S COLLECTION)

Before starting west, young miners joked about "going to see the elephant," meaning that they were ready for the risks and adventures on the trail and in the gold fields. Later, usually homesick and broke, many headed home, claiming they had seen "the elephant's tail."

California, plus instructions from friends and relatives, directed people to wood, grass, water, and cutoffs. Messages were posted on boards or on the animal bones that lined the trail.

John McWilliams, age sixteen, left Illinois for California in an all-male wagon train. Near present-day Redding, California, John worked a rocker, made of a hollowed-out log, and mined for gold. His friends called him "legs-a-might," because John was a skinny six feet one-and-a-half inches tall. Many different races of people from around the world worked side by side, panning for gold. On the first day, John and his fellow miners found one hundred dollars' worth of gold. Most of the time, they found nothing.

The boom year was 1852, when $81 million worth of gold was mined from northern California's earth. A seventeen-year-old miner, Jasper Smith Hill, panned along the American River, where Marshall had discovered gold. Once in a while, he washed out fifty cents to several dollars' worth of gold in his pan. He often wrote his family back home in Iowa, saying, "There's a chance of making money yet in California." Jasper never actually struck pay dirt.

Some emigrants headed to California on the Old Spanish Trail. From Santa Fe, New Mexico, this trail looped through a corner of Colorado, into Utah, across the tip of Nevada, and into California and the city of Los Angeles. The Gila Trail (also called the Southern Emigrant Trail) started in New Mexico and went across the sandy Arizona desert to San Diego in southern California. Besides gold, these emigrants came for farmland and warm weather.

The Hall family from Texas stopped at army forts, such as Fort Yuma in Arizona, and at trading stations to buy supplies. Nine-year-old

Maggie Hall recalled crossing the Gila River several times, with her father swimming the stock across by holding on to their horns. "The Yuma Indians were lost in admiration of Pa," remembered Maggie, "[and] his size and feats of swimming."

The desert was hot and dry. Sometimes it was easier to travel in the cool parts of the day. The dust was thick and almost unbearable. It was long and boring—not quick, as some newspaper advertisements had promised.

Maggie wrote about the heat, dying oxen, and no water during one part of her journey to California. "The sandstorm that . . . came . . . was a terrible experience. . . . Neither horses nor oxen would go against it and the men could not expose their faces. . . . The stock huddled

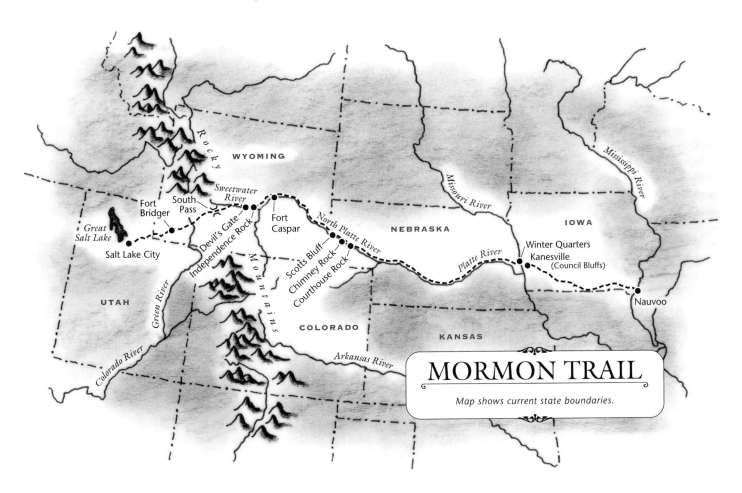

MORMON TRAIL

Map shows current state boundaries.

THE MORMON TRAIL

The Mormon Trail was the only route related to a religion. Members of the Church of Jesus Christ of Latter-day Saints, or Mormons, led by Brigham Young and his prophets, began to migrate west in 1846. The Saints, as they also were called, were searching for a new place to live after being persecuted for their religious beliefs.

They fled across the Missouri River, following the north side of the Platte River, and headed toward the Rocky Mountains. They found Zion—the promised land—in the Salt Lake Valley area, now present-day Utah. Mormon families moved to Salt Lake City by covered wagon, animal-drawn carts, and carriages. After creating an extensive irrigation system, they were able to turn the dry desert into an agricultural oasis.

Starting in 1856, more Mormons came to the United States from around the world. After reaching the Midwest, many filled handcarts—which looked like oversized wheelbarrows—with food and other essentials. Fully loaded, some carts weighed four hundred pounds. Numerous handcart companies crossed the plains between 1856 and 1860. It was hard work pushing or pulling a cart ten to twenty miles a day in heat and in blizzards. Nearly one in ten handcart travelers died en route. More died at the end of the trail, in Salt Lake City, worn out from the trip.

Thousands of Mormons migrated to Utah in what was called "the gathering" and made Salt Lake City their new home. Both Mormons and non-Mormons used the Mormon Trail until the coming of the railroad.

together. . . . Mother and children stayed in the wagon and we had no supper that night."

When the easy-to-find gold was gone in California, miners found different work or headed to other areas to look for gold and other precious metals. Three hundred million dollars' worth of silver and gold were mined from Nevada's Comstock Lode. Gold was also discovered in Colorado, then in the Black Hills of South Dakota.

Mormon families were gathering on both sides of the Missouri River. By the end of 1846, about seven thousand Mormons lived either in Miller's Hollow (later called Kanesville and Council Bluffs) on the

Mormon travelers used wagons or handcarts to carry their important belongings as they fled religious persecution, as depicted in this reenactment event.

Iowa side of the Missouri River or in Winter Quarters, near present-day Omaha, on the Nebraska side. They formed wagon trains to go one thousand miles to the Great Salt Lake Valley.

They began to flee west in 1847 in search of religious freedom, following the north bank of the Platte River. After leaving South Pass, they headed southwest to Fort Bridger, then went one hundred miles to the valley of the Great Salt Lake. This new route was called the Mormon Trail, although it had actually been blazed by fur traders in the 1830s.

The Mormons made trail improvements to help other families en route to the Salt Lake area. They built log shelters along the way and planted crops there. Mormon travelers carried a twenty-four-page booklet, "The Latter-Day Saints' Emigrant Guide," by William

Clayton, for information about food, water, wood, hazards, landmarks, forts, mileage, and more.

By August 1847, some 450 Mormons inhabited what is now called Salt Lake City in the future state of Utah. Within a short time, they had built a large irrigation system to bring water to the area. Because of the water, the Mormons became successful desert farmers, and the city grew.

Later wagon trains would detour to Salt Lake City to rest for a few days and to trade for goods. As one ten-year-old wrote, "We saw Salt Lake at a distance, and when the sun shone on it, it looked like a lake of gold. We camped for a week [nearby]. Every block had a stream of clear, sparkling water running around it. We purchased fresh vegetables . . . and they were the best we had ever tasted."

Wherever they were—en route to California, Oregon, Utah, or somewhere else—pioneers of all ages found it hard to write letters or update their diaries during their busy days on the trail. "We are rather tired when we stop and do not feel much like writing," penned a young man in a letter to his mother. Exhausted though they were, many pioneers did write about their experiences. Many of them felt that they were making history and that it was important to keep a record for future generations.

The roads west were crowded following California's gold rush. In 1860, California had nearly four hundred thousand people. Oregon had fifty-two thousand and Utah had forty thousand that year. And by 1870, nearly seventy thousand Mormons had settled in Salt Lake City.

This large wagon train carried Mormon families toward Salt Lake City. (LDS CHURCH ARCHIVES)

Chapter Seven

ENTERTAINMENT AND CELEBRATIONS

Day after day, wagon trains slowly rolled west. During the busy years on the trail, like 1849, wagon trains would travel for days near other groups. One train would stop to rest and the other line of wagons would pull ahead, only to be passed by the first group a few days later. Some trains might meet again after many days, and others never again.

Children played with their dolls and toys in the wagons or while sitting on the spring seats. Older children were sometimes allowed to ride on the wagon tongue with a hand resting on the oxen on either side, though this was dangerous. They also walked beside the wagons, collecting rocks, turtles, and other treasures. If they had ponies, children stuffed these treasures into their saddlebags. One boy wrote:

> This [trip] was a real picnic to my nine year old mind . . . and I was afraid of missing something. I would run ahead of the pokey oxen, not far enough for an Indian to grab me, however, and pick flowers, gather fuel, or whatever came to mind. I seldom walked less than ten or fifteen miles a day. I was thin and tall for my age and if I was tired at night I do not remember it.

At the nooning, while adults rested and animals grazed, young people might wade in creeks. As Eliza Donner remembered, she and her playmates would "make mud pies, and gather posies in the narrow glades between the . . . trees." Older friends played chess and board games like Mansion of Happiness.

One day, Harriet Hitchcock's family camped beside "a beautiful little stream." Harriet wrote that "for a change I have been wandering around among the bushes until I found a birds nest, with five blue eggs in it looking for all the world just as birds eggs look at home."

Harriet, with the help of her sister, Lucy, caught a prairie dog and kept it in a cage. "In order to tame it, I take it out every day and feed it with meat."

Prairie dogs dig deep tunnels in the dirt. Burrowing owls raise their young in abandoned underground runs, and snakes and other reptiles often escape the heat or cold in prairie dog towns.
(L. Tom Perry Special Collections, Harold B. Lee Library, Brigham Young University/William Henry Jackson)

MANSION OF HAPPINESS

The Mansion of Happiness, America's first popular board game, initially produced in 1843, went west with many pioneer families.

The game appealed to teenagers, who sat around the board and took turns spinning an eight-sided wooden top. Mansion of Happiness combined play with moral lessons. Players moved from square to square, hoping to reach the center of the board—Eternal Happiness. Along the way, they might land on squares for Honesty, Sincerity, and Generosity or be penalized for landing on squares for Poverty, Cruelty, and Ingratitude. Reaching a Robber square, the player went to prison for two turns. A Drunkard wound up in the Stocks.

A mother traveling from Wisconsin to California in 1853 wrote in her diary at South Pass in the Rocky Mountains that her daughter and friends "are enjoying themselves with their guitars and the 'Mansion of Happiness,' etc. etc., and are a lively, pleasant group indeed."

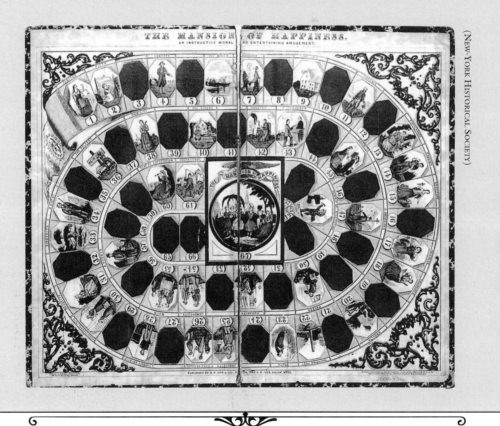

Jesse Applegate was also interested in prairie dogs, with their barking and their huge homes of connecting mounds and openings. He recalled that

> as we pass through or near their towns they would come up out of their holes and sit up straight on their hind quarters, always near their burrow, and utter something like a yelp, or so it seemed to me, and on the slightest alarm drop into their holes. I saw owls sitting among them, and it was said that prairie dogs, owls, and rattlesnakes lived together in the same holes.

It was fun to play sports, too. Jesse recalled when an ox was slaughtered at camp and the gutted stomach swelled up to the size of a barrel. He and his friends liked

> running and butting the head against the swollen paunch and being bounced back . . . and [we had a contest to see] who could butt the harder. [One boy named Andy] came down like a pile driver against the paunch, but he did not bounce back. We . . . discovered that Andy has thrust his head into the stomach, which had closed so tightly around his neck that he could not withdraw his head. We took hold of his legs and pulled him out.

Another popular pastime was to play soldiers and Indians. Eliza Ann McAuley practiced target shooting with her brother's pistol. "I was very expert at missing the mark," she wrote in her diary. It was also fun to have "snowball" fights with dried buffalo chips and to try to see who could sail them the farthest.

Like Harriet, Eliza Ann had a wild pet, a pronghorn antelope she named Jennie. In July, the wagon train was camped beside a river, near a party of Indians. Indian dogs chased Jennie and killed her. The Indians were upset and tried to give Eliza Ann skins and robes for what had happened. "We told them it was an accident and they were not to blame, but they immediately packed up to go, saying they were afraid the men [in the wagon train] would shoot them."

Harriet's prairie dog died in an accident, when the wagon tipped over in the mountains. "Ma's rocking chair was crushed. . . . The pail of milk for our dinner spilled and our poor little prairie dog went rolling in his cage to the foot of the mountain."

There wasn't much time to grieve over the death of a pet. Children were just too busy playing, helping their parents, or exploring. Many of the young people climbed to the top of Independence Rock and, at Steamboat Springs in Idaho, watched steam spout from the ground. Sometimes they plugged the exit hole with dirt or grass, then watched

Solomon Butcher, a well-known western photographer, took this picture of emigrants at a "post office" on the trail. There was probably a barrel or box nearby where they could leave messages or get instructions.
(NEBRASKA STATE HISTORICAL SOCIETY)

everything blow skyward. When one boy set his hat over the hole, the pressure blew the top off the hat.

Some pioneers liked to draw and read. Popular books were *The Life of Daniel Boone*, *Pilgrim's Progress,* and *Robinson Crusoe*. For entertainment, Virginia Reed wrote letters home. "How I enjoyed riding my pony [Billy], galloping over the plain gathering wildflowers!"

For thirteen-year-old Virginia and the other letter writers, there were lots of "prairie post offices." Messages were scrawled on scraps of paper or cloth and pinned to a stick beside the trail or at popular campsites. Pioneers carved messages on tree trunks or painted them on rocks. One traveler recalled passing a wooden barrel with "Post Office" painted on it. Most of the mail was for emigrants in the rear, to hurry them along, to mention cutoffs, or to give family news.

Even the smooth, white bones of dead animals or people were perfect places to leave information. Martha Gay, also thirteen, wrote in 1851 that "we would pick them up [the bones] and read verses which some passerby had written on them, then perhaps add a line or two." It was also cheering to find a relative or a friend's name carved in a tree trunk or in a soft, sandstone cliff. Later travelers were able to mail letters from real post offices at Fort Kearny, Fort Laramie, or Salt Lake City.

Each wagon had an evening cooking fire, and after a meal, everyone gathered around the fires. "The men," Marion Russell recalled, "would tell stories of the strange new land before us, tales of gold and Indians. The women would sit with their long skirts drawn up over a sleeping child on their laps. . . . The little camp fires flickered, and behind us loomed the dark hulks of the covered wagons."

Around the campfire, scouts often told tales of adventure and hardship. Joe Meek told how, when he was close to starving to death, he had held his "hands in an ant hill until they were covered with ants, then greedily licked them off. I have taken the soles of my moccasins, crisped them in the fire, and eaten them."

Pioneers often wrote messages or warnings to other travelers on the sun-bleached bones of dead animals and left them beside the trail.

(AUTHOR'S COLLECTION)

Children—and parents—stayed awake when he said that he and his fellow mountain men "used to take a kettle of hot water, catch the crickets and throw them in, and when they stopped kicking, eat them."

Peg Leg Smith, an old mountaineer who had a cabin along the trail, hobbled into another camp on his wooden leg. He told the pioneers that years before, he had injured his leg in the wilderness. Gangrene set in, and Peg Leg knew what he had to do . . . or die. He got out his knife and amputated his leg.

Besides listening to stories and tall tales, children visited one another's wagons or wagon trains camped nearby. They played ball and other games by moonlight or enjoyed music. Nearly every wagon train had one or two musicians, and that led to dancing and singing. While teenager Maria Elliott worked on her embroidery one evening in 1859, dozens of campfires sparkled in the night, and a man from another wagon train "came over and played the violin and some sang. He is a first rate player. There were fifty-one sitting round to hear the music until quite late."

Wherever there happened to be a smooth piece of ground, pioneers didn't miss the chance to dance to a country reel or jig to fiddle music after supper, especially during the early, and relatively easy, travel on the trail. Sometimes birthdays were celebrated. Kate McDaniel's mother made animal-shaped cookies for her father's birthday. "We cherished our little cookies. . . . But finally we [took] just a wee taste; so few sweets did we get those days. We would just take a bit of a nibble like mice. We would try to make them last as long as possible."

Every day—and night—was different. Eliza Ann McAuley wrote in her journal that just after dark "we were treated to a variety of barnyard music. . . . Roosters crowed, hens cackled, ducks quacked, pigs squealed, owls hooted, donkeys brayed, dogs howled, cats squalled and all these perfect imitations were made by the human voice." Mules, oxen, cows, and horses grazed nearby, to the sounds of a tinkling animal bell or two.

During the long trip, young people fell in and out of love. John, a teenager en route to Oregon, flirted with a sixteen-year-old girl in his wagon train. But her father disapproved, and, according to one story, he took his wagon and family to another, nearby train. The two young sweethearts left each other love notes by using false names and writing on buffalo skulls at the side of the trail.

Marriages took place, and they were recorded in journal entries like this one in 1847: "Wedding in camp this night, and a very tall spree

Emigrants gather at the end of the day to cook, play games, and rest.

[a lively party].” Rebecca Nutting, who was fourteen when she started west from Iowa, described the prairie wedding of a family friend. After the ceremony,

> the newly married couple occupied a wagon for sleeping apartments. The first notice that they had of any disturbance was when the [men and women] took hold of the wagon . . . and ran the wagon a half mile out on the prairie. Then the fun began. Such banging of cans shooting of guns, etc, and every noice conceivable was resorted to . . . until midnight . . . leaving the happy couple out on the prairie . . . until morning when they came walking into camp amid cheers and congratulations.

The Fourth of July was a very important day on the trail. Pioneers thought of family and friends back home. And most wagon trains honored Independence Day with some kind of feast or event. If they happened to be at Independence Rock, the halfway point, pioneers even danced on top of the landmark. If another train was nearby, the two groups might celebrate together. Maria Elliott’s diary entry on July 4, 1859, stated:

> I was awakened this morning bright and early by the firing of guns from some distant [wagon] companies. It seems that they had not forgotten Independence Day [even] if they were far away on the plains, and from home and friends. Got breakfast quite early, but before breakfast the boys fired off some shooters. Had apple dumplings for supper which were very good. We had an invitation . . . to a Fourth of July dance. . . . After supper, [brother] Jack played on the violin, and some of the boys sang before retiring.

Another young pioneer wrote on the Fourth of July, “This is a delightful morning a few sweet birds are trying to sing their makers praise. . . . Our thoughts are continuously turning homeward. . . . I suppose your all haveing a sabbath school celebration to day. . . . We would like to take a sly squint and see what you are doing.”

Some wagon trains didn't celebrate the Fourth of July. It was entirely up to the captain. Some preferred to push on, especially if they had already stopped for the birth of a child, to fix a broken wagon, or other such time-consuming event. No one wanted to cross the mountains in the winter.

On July 3, Helen Carpenter noted in her diary that they finally reached a "camping place after dark." Her uncle Sam had already started a fire. Everyone was tired, and "some of us were cross and wet." The next morning, the group discovered that the campfire was on a grave. They didn't bother to move the fire, and Helen commented on "our growing indifference . . . and that what we are . . . to endure each day is robbing us of all sentiment."

They packed up. It was warm on the trail, and there were mosquitoes. Helen wrote that "this has not seemed at all like 'Independence Day' but just the same old jolts with plenty of dust thrown in."

Chapter Eight

CHORES AND CHOW

Most children were used to doing farm chores, having started almost as soon as they could walk. On the trail, girls washed clothes, cooked, and scrubbed the pots and pans with sand. They cared for their younger brothers and sisters, too. Mary Field, who was sixteen, had many jobs. She helped her mother with the other children and cooked. Every day, she walked beside the oxen and encouraged them to keep going, since she "had to walk most of the way across the plains [to Utah] because there was not enough room in the wagon for all of us."

Everyone—children and adults—hauled water to camp at the end of the day. Boys fed and watered the animals, milked the cows, and hunted with their fathers. Older children helped pitch the tents at night and hitch up the oxen each morning. Boys as young as twelve years old were expected to stand guard at night, even in rain, hail, or dust storms. They watched for Indians and made sure the stock didn't stray too far.

Charley True, a sixteen-year-old in 1859, remembered guard duty and that he "stood watch alone with the unearthly howls of the coyotes breaking the silence . . . and an intense awareness of the beauty of the moonlit landscape." Another night, he was eating dinner and ready for bed. "We heard no disturbance whatever. Then [we discovered] every hoof was gone. . . . They had gone from us in the darkness . . . swallowed up by the earth."

Mornings started early, even for boys and men who had been awake all night guarding animals. Tired as he was, Charley still had to find the missing animals. Marion Russell recalled other mornings when

> men began rolling out from under the wagons. Soon breakfast fires were burning and the men were catching and harnessing the mules. Through partially closed tent flaps and wagon curtains women could be seen slipping their dresses on. . . . Children cried at being forced out from under warm blankets. I found it hard to button all the buttons that ran up and down the back of my dress. Why couldn't they have been put on front where I could get at them? Dressed and out in the sunshine we were all happy.

After a few weeks on the trail, no one wore fancy clothes. Skirts, petticoats, and pants were tattered and torn from sagebrush and cactus. Travelers tossed out good clothes, including impractical hoop skirts. They packed up white collars and cuffs that had to be washed, starched, and ironed.

Most of the men stopped shaving. They grew tan and leathery looking in the dry air. No one bathed every day. Rivers, like the muddy Platte River, weren't very inviting. Some days, there was hardly enough time—or clean water—to wash faces and hands. Marion said that "Mother, Will, and I had to wash our faces and hands in the same basin of water. Will washed last, for Mother said he was the dirtiest."

Following breakfast, "the children were counted and loaded. A swift glance about to see that nothing was left behind and we were off for another day on the trail," Marion said. Drivers climbed aboard, with

*The driver flicked his whip and
called out "gee" and "haw" to
keep his animals moving.*
(Denver Public Library,
Western History Collection)

whips in hand. Charles Young, who was heading to Colorado in 1865,
wrote:

> The whips consisted of a hickory stalk two feet long, a lash twelve
> feet in length with a buck or antelope skin snapper nine inches in
> length. The stalk was held in the left hand, the lash coiled with the
> right hand and index finger of the left. It was then whirled several
> times around the head, letting it shoot straight out and bringing it
> back with a quick jerk. It would strike wherever aimed, raising a
> deadhead ox nearly off its hind quarters and cutting through the
> hide and into the flesh. When thrown into space, it would make a
> report nearly as loud as a revolver.

Since the wagons moved at a walking pace, children could jump
down to gather berries along streams and river banks. While the wagon

bounced along, they might roll out a pie crust on the wagon seat or help their mothers peel potatoes for the next meal.

The wagon trains stopped at noon, mainly to rest the animals. Helen Carpenter wrote that in her train "we often eat bread and milk at noon more than anything else. The milk is carried in a can swung to the wagon bows overhead. By noon (if the churn works well and seldom fails), there is a little ball of butter the size of a hickory nut and innumerable little ones." By night, they had more butter and buttermilk, to be used as part of the evening's meal.

Hunting was a job for the men and boys, and they searched for deer, antelope, and buffalo. In the early years of the migration, John Bidwell

Preparing the noon meal on a drop-down table attached to the back of the wagon.
(MUSEUM OF NEW MEXICO/ T. HARMON PARKHURST)

BUFFALO

American bison, or buffalo, as they are commonly called, once roamed the plains between the Canadian prairies and the Rio Grande. They herded together in groups of hundreds to tens of thousands to millions.

Indians hunted them and used the buffalo for food, shelter, clothing, and much more. For the non-native hunter, the buffalo meant money. Buffalo hunters killed the shaggy animals for their hides.

Two men could handle twenty-five carcasses each day. They'd slit the hide along the belly from the throat to the tip of the tail and down each leg to eight inches above the hoof. Each animal was skinned out and, with the help of a horse or team, the hide was pulled free. It wasn't easy. Male buffalo weigh up to two thousand pounds.

Wolves, vultures, and other carnivores feasted on the rotting remains. Fertilizer companies gathered the bones. In Kansas alone, between 1868 and 1881, the bones of thirty-one million buffalo were ground into fertilizer.

Early emigrants passed the stinking hide-filled wagons of buffalo hunters. The men were hurrying to ship the hides east by steamboat and railroad. They sold for three dollars apiece.

The United States government encouraged the killing of buffalo to hurt the Indian tribes who depended on them for survival. Then the pioneers could more easily claim Indian territory for their own use.

By the end of the nineteenth century, the vast buffalo herds were gone. And the buffalo were in danger of becoming extinct.

wrote that along the Platte River "I saw . . . in one day more buffaloes than I have ever seen of cattle in all my life. I have seen the plains black with them for several days' journey as far as the eye could reach."

Following the practice of some white hunters, members of the Bidwell Party killed the huge animals for the tongues, hump meat, and marrow bones, leaving the rest on the prairie for the wolves to eat. Bidwell wrote that the Cheyenne Indians, "who traveled ahead of us for two or three days, set us a better example. At their camps we noticed that they took all the [buffalo] meat, everything but the bones."

Marion Russell said in her memoirs that "our trail often led among herds of buffalo so numerous that at times we were half afraid." The moving, dark masses of buffalo made a low, rumbling sound, like an approaching earthquake. At times, the men and boys had to fire their guns to keep the huge herds from running through the wagon trains and trampling everything in their path.

Helen Carpenter described how her brothers and husband, "some on foot, some on horseback, armed with muskets, revolvers and knives," chased a small band of buffalo. They shot a male buffalo about two miles from the train. Ten oxen dragged the dead animal to camp. Helen's nine-year-old brother, Hale, stood by the shoulders and "his head could not be seen from the opposite side."

They roasted the tender parts first, then dried the rest. Helen wrote that "the wagons are decorated with slices of meat dangling from

Buffalo hunters in Sheridan, Kansas, around 1874. Note the skins drying on the rack and the large pile of bones in the far distance.
(Kansas State Historical Society)

A single gunshot or a clap of thunder might cause a grazing herd of buffalo to stampede straight toward a wagon train.
(WESTERN HISTORY COLLECTIONS, UNIVERSITY OF OKLAHOMA LIBRARY/ W. S. CAMPBELL)

strings fastened to ropes that reach from front to back along the side of the wagons, looking very much like coarse red fringe." The women made soups and stews with bones and meat scraps, flavored with wild onions.

Along the way, emigrants also ate berries, waterfowl, turkeys, and fish. Young people liked to fish. Elisha Brooks put grasshoppers on his hook and fished in the Humboldt River in Nevada. Eleven-year-old George Goodridge, with his sister, Sophia, tried out the Green River in Wyoming. "We spent the day fishing. Caught some beautiful large trout," Sophia reported.

It was not always easy to shoot enough food. When they couldn't find anything else, the men tried to pick off prairie dogs. One man put in his diary that they were very difficult to kill, and unless shot thro' head—though nearly cut in half,—with entrails out, and [several] yards from their hole, will manage to get down before you can run up & seize them—Have caught them by tail & jerked out of hole,—dead, and so mutilated as to be worthless.

Sometimes they roasted jack rabbits or "bush trout," another name for rattlesnake meat. Helen wasn't sure she wanted to eat the ground squirrels her brother shot, saying, "I am firm in the belief that they are *rats*. I protested against cooking rats, but fresh meat has been so scarce. . . . They tasted too much like fish to ever become very popular."

Sallie Hester put in her diary that "we live on bacon, ham, rice, dried fruits, molasses, packed butter, bread, coffee, tea, and milk as we have our own cows." Not everyone brought milk cows. Or if they did, their cows might stop producing milk or even die along the way.

Charley True's milk cow, Starry, was tan, with one crumpled horn and a white star on her forehead. At first, she tried to run away and go back home. When Starry was roped to the back of the wagon, she would go stiff legged and fall over. Finally, Starry was put in a wooden yoke with Betty, another milk cow. They were hitched up behind the team of oxen, and the stronger animals dragged them along to California.

Like Sallie's family, the Brookses also had dried fruit, which didn't take much space in the wagon. When no one was looking, Elisha got into his family's supply of apples. "From my experience I can recommend dried apples as an economical diet: you need but one meal a day; you can eat dried apples for breakfast, drink water for dinner and swell for supper."

Families also depended on dried meat and other kinds of staples. Benjamin Bonney said that his family carried "a lot of pickled pork . . . [and] over a hundred pounds of maple sugar . . . [and] plenty of corn meal. . . . [Father] laid in a plentiful supply of home twist tobacco. Father chewed it and mother smoked it . . . in an old corn cob pipe."

Once, Benjamin recorded in his memoirs, his family camped near some Indians who shared their food. They ate some blackish bread that resembled fruitcake but, after taking a closer look, realized that the Indians had made a loaf of ground acorns and crickets.

Emigrants had a hard time collecting enough fuel for their fires. In the early years of the migration, they cut down and burned the trees along the river valleys. Abandoned wagons, oxen yokes, and even books became firewood in later years.

Edwin Pettit, age thirteen, picked up buffalo chips, watching carefully for any rattlesnakes coiled beneath them. When her wagon train stopped, Marion Russell walked out onto the prairie to "gather the buffalo chips [for the cooking fires]. I would stand back and kick them,

Ada McColl and her little brother, Burt, who is wearing what is most likely a hand-me-down dress, are collecting buffalo chips on the prairie.
(Kansas State Historical Society)

Pioneers often saw or heard coyotes and wolves. Today wolves no longer live along most of the trail routes.
(THE HUNTINGTON LIBRARY)

then reach down and gather them carefully, for under them lived big spiders and centipedes. Sometimes scorpions ran from beneath them. I would fill my long full dress skirt with the evening's fuel and take it back to mother."

Some children took on even bigger jobs. Jasper Henry Lawn was in a group going to California. His father had died in Illinois, so Jasper drove the family's wagon from start to finish. He was only ten years old. Mary Ellen Todd loved to drive and crack the whip. She wrote in her diary on her way to Oregon that there was "a secret joy in being able to have a power that set things going."

After a long day, Edwin, Marion, Benjamin, Sallie, Jasper, and the other children had no trouble falling asleep. Marion admitted that "sometimes in the night I would awaken to hear the coyote's eerie cry in the darkness. I would creep close to mother and shiver." And then she would drift off to sleep again.

Chapter Nine

LIFE, DEATH, AND ACCIDENTS

About one out of every seventeen pioneers ended up in a grave beside the trail. "Died of Cholera" was the most frequent grave marker. Disease, not Indian attacks, caused the highest number of deaths. The routes were marked with wooden crosses and stone cairns. People died without doctors, without ministers, and sometimes even without friends.

Many women brought medicines from home, and they expected to do most of the doctoring. As thirteen-year-old Martha Ann Morrison, who traveled west in 1844, recalled, "The mothers had the families directly in their hands and were with them all the time, especially during sickness."

Lucy Ann Henderson, age eleven, was going to Oregon with her parents, brothers, and sisters. "Mother . . . hung the bag containing the medicine from a nail on a sideboard of the wagon." A typical bag held quinine for malaria, hartshorn (ammonia powder) for snake bites, laudanum as a painkiller, and citric acid for scurvy, resulting from a diet lacking in vitamin C. One mother suggested it include "a bottle of physicking pills [laxatives], a quart of castor oil, a quart of the best rum, and a large vial of peppermint essences [for stomach upsets]."

Women read about cures in almanacs and wrote these remedies in their cookbooks, Bibles, and journals. They mixed their own medicines, using common ingredients like flour, bread, eggs, sugar, onions, honey, mustard, whiskey, kerosene, turpentine, hay, corn, animal grease, manure, bacon, weeds, and garden herbs.

One way to prevent a cold, some people believed, was to wear garlic around the neck. To cure a sore throat, one could eat a mix of kerosene and sugar. Another popular cure was to wrap a sore throat with a dirty sock. According to one pioneer, the sock must be still warm from the foot.

There wasn't time to rest. A sick child had to lie in the back of the bouncing wagon. Older girls might nurse their sick brothers and sisters, or even their parents, in a moving wagon. Maria Elliott recalled that when her brother, Charley, was bitten by a scorpion, the "poison was all over his hands. They gave him a shot of . . . brandy and put a tobacco poultice on the bite. He was crazy for about three or four hours, and then fell asleep." It may have been Maria's job to watch over him. If she had to, Maria could also fix gunshot wounds and splint broken legs.

One of five women who went west was pregnant. Women were expected to be prepared to give birth on the trail and, it was hoped, not to delay the train for more than a day.

When Catherine Sager's mother went into labor, the wagon train camped near a river for the night. It was raining and cold. The baby girl was born in a damp canvas tent. It was not an easy birth, and everyone waited for Mrs. Sager to improve. Two days later, the wagons moved out. At the

Children had to swallow spoonfuls of cod liver oil, a yellow liquid made from fish livers, to cure a variety of ailments. It tasted horrible!
(AUTHOR'S COLLECTION)

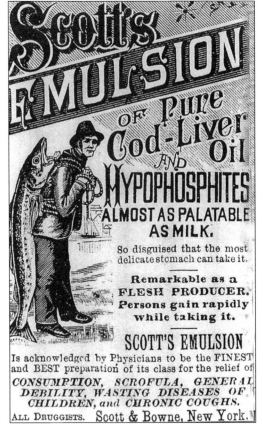

age of nine, Catherine was the oldest daughter, and she was expected to care for her little sisters while her mother rested with the baby in the wagon.

Adrietta Hixon, en route to Oregon with her parents, was surprised by the birth of a baby brother on the trail. At first, all she noticed was that

> Father did some washing and extra cooking that day. . . . Later that evening I heard Father ask Mother what she thought about going on the next day. She answered "the baby and I can ride as well on this feather bed as not." The next morning we slowly moved out, often stopping on the way so that Father might attend to mother and the little Elijah.

People didn't know much about sanitation or how diseases were spread. As more and more wagon trains took the same trails, pioneers left behind campsites that were increasingly filthy with human and animal waste, garbage, and dead animals.

Cholera, which is spread by contaminated water, infested many cities east of the Missouri River. As families fled west, they brought cholera with them. Cholera epidemics moved through the wagon trains, especially in the years 1848 to 1852. When Marion Russell and her family left Fort Leavenworth, "Tar barrels were burning in the streets . . . to ward off the cholera, and clouds of black smoke drifted over us as we pulled out."

Cholera struck hard and fast, with diarrhea, vomiting, fever, chills, cramps, convulsions, and often death. A person could be fine in the morning, have terrible stomach pains a few hours later, and die that night. And death was so certain that companions would dig graves before the dying person was actually gone.

Ash Hollow was one of the best-known Oregon-California Trail landmarks because of its springs and cedar and ash trees. After long

REMEDIES FOR
CHOLERA

As prescribed by the Edinburgh Board of Health, and approved of by the Faculty of New-York.

CAREFULLY PREPARED BY JEFFERSON B. NONES,
APOTHECARY AND CHEMIST,
NO. 644½ BROADWAY, NEW-YORK.

NO. 1.–CHOLERA MIXTURE.

A table-spoonful with 60 drops of Laudanum, in half a wine-glassful of cold water. If this fail to relieve, repeat two spoonsful, with 30 drops of Laudanum every half hour. Half these doses of mixture and laudanum, for children of 14. One-fourth for children of 7. Do not exceed the doses prescribed; and stop when the vomiting and cramps cease, unless you have medical advice.

NO. 2.–BOTTLE OF LAUDANUM.

NO. 3.–CHOLERA PILLS.

To be used if the mixture No. 1 be vomited. Two pills at first, and then one every half hour, if the first fail to relieve. Half these doses for children of 14; one-fourth for children of 7. Do not exceed the doses prescribed, and stop when the vomiting and cramp cease, unless you have medical advice.

NO. 4.–CHOLERA CLYSTERS.

Inject three tea-spoonsful in a wine-glassful of thin warm gruel, and retain as long as possible by pressure below with a warm cloth; if not retained, repeat immediately, but otherwise not. Half the dose for children of 14—one fourth for children of 7.

NO. 5.–MUSTARD POULTICES.

A fourth part is enough for one person. Dust it thickly over porridge poultices, of which apply a large one on the belly, and others on the soles and calves. Remove when the patient complains much of the smarting.

Greenwich Printing Office, 118 Barrow-street.

This list of cholera treatments was published about 1835. Cholera was the biggest cause of death on the trails. (NEW-YORK HISTORICAL SOCIETY)

days on the dry plains, pioneers looked forward to this site in the middle of Nebraska. During the gold rush stampede, the trees were cut down and the springs were polluted. Ash Hollow became a cemetery, primarily for victims of cholera.

Other illnesses, like measles, scarlet fever, and whooping cough, killed many young children. Emigrants also died from mumps, tuberculosis, dysentery, typhoid, malaria, and smallpox. A red flag flying from a wagon indicated the presence of smallpox, a contagious disease. Everyone stayed away.

Indians often dug up graves, looking for blankets, clothing, or personal belongings. Unknowingly, these grave robbers were exposed to cholera, smallpox, and other infectious diseases and took the deadly germs back to their people. These diseases could kill an entire Indian village.

On some sections of the trail, later travelers saw fresh graves every hundred yards. Eliza Ann McAuley wrote in her journal that her group crossed the Sweetwater River and "here we saw the graves of . . . two sisters, acquaintances of ours, on their way to Oregon."

Most emigrants had no wood for coffins, so they wrapped the dead in cloth and, if possible, buried them under rocks and hard-packed dirt. Some graves were dug in the ruts of the wagon trail so that the wagons would roll over the dirt and wolves and Indians would not be able to find them. One emigrant saw a piece of a woman's hair sticking out of the trail with the comb still in it.

Catherine Sager almost died just before her train reached Fort Laramie. As she had done many times before, Catherine leaped from the moving wagon. Her skirt caught on an ax handle and she was swept under the wagon. A wheel rolled over her leg, crushing it in several places. For weeks, she lay in the jolting wagon bed, waiting for her broken bones to grow back together. It would take a year for her leg to fully mend.

Seven-year-old Enoch Garrison wasn't as lucky. He liked to stand on the wagon tongue and help drive the oxen. His father kept telling him it was too dangerous. Enoch didn't listen, and he was thrown under the wheels. One wheel smashed his leg. A week later, gangrene set in.

RACHEL PATTISON

The most famous grave at Ash Hollow, Nebraska, is that of eighteen-year-old Rachel Pattison. Rachel was coming west from Illinois with Nathan, her husband of just two months. Nathan wrote in his diary on June 19, 1849, that Rachel was sick in the morning and died that night of cholera.

The wagon train buried Rachel at the entrance to Ash Hollow and marked the spot with a stone. They left the next day. Other pioneers, after seeing Rachel's grave, wrote in their own journals about the sad and sudden death of the young bride.

Today Rachel's grave site is visible, but the other early graves have vanished. Over time, wolves and coyotes dug up graves, and weather—wind, rain, and flood—washed away most markers. The original stone that Nathan placed on his wife's grave has been encased in a larger monument.

Wagon wheel ruts still cut into the steep hillside leading down to Ash Hollow.

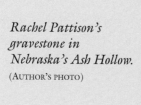

Rachel Pattison's gravestone in Nebraska's Ash Hollow.
(AUTHOR'S PHOTO)

Two rock-covered graves on the Oregon Trail, dated 1844 and 1845, in present-day Wyoming.
(WYOMING STATE ARCHIVES)

The train stopped, and Enoch was given some laudanum, a kind of opium, to ease the pain. During emergency surgery to take off the leg, Enoch died.

Surgery, like Enoch's, was rare during the migration years and done only as a last resort. Charles Young remembered in 1865 that there was no anesthetic, and tools were "a knife sharpened as keen as a razor's edge. . . . Another [knife] hacked into a saw would separate the bones and sensitive marrow; while an iron [rod] heated to a white heat seared up the arteries and the trick was done."

While the Sagers' wagon train crossed the Rocky Mountains, a sickness known as "camp fever" struck, killing three people, including Catherine's father. That same day he was buried beside a river, and the train continued west.

The wagons reached Oregon Territory and followed a dusty trail along the Snake River. In the middle of September, Catherine's mother turned sick with the same fever, which may have been typhoid, another infectious, often fatal disease. Mrs. Sager prayed that she would make it to the Whitman Mission, where she and the children could spend the winter.

"We traveled over a very rough road, and she moaned pitifully all day," recalled Catherine. Her mother died that night. The children wrapped her in a sheet and buried her along the trail. A wooden board marked the spot. "The teams were then hitched to the wagon and the train drove on . . . and we were orphans, the oldest fourteen years old and the youngest five months old," Catherine wrote in her memoirs.

Mary Ackley lost her mother while traveling west. So did the Scott children in 1852. Seventeen-year-old Abigail Jane Scott, or Jenny, as her family called her, wrote in the family journal that her mother died of cholera on June 20. The family buried Ann Scott in a shallow grave

Death often came quickly on the trail because there were limited medicines, few doctors, and no hospitals. Just as quickly, the dead were buried and the wagon train moved on.
(THE BANCROFT LIBRARY, UNIVERSITY OF CALIFORNIA BERKELEY)

on a feather mattress, then covered her with stones. Jenny wrote that "the grave . . . overlooks small pine and cedar trees . . . clusters of wild roses and various other wild flowers grow in abundance . . . [and there] reposes the last earthly remains of *my mother.*"

Snake and insect bites, burns, and cuts were common. So were shootings, near drownings, or accidents from being around animals. One grave marker read:

Two Children Killed by a Stampede
June 23, 1864

There were injuries from knife fights and gunfights, when men were pushed to the edge because of hardship on the trail. A bride wrote to her sister that "our men are all well armed. William carries a brace of pistols and a bowie knife. Ain't that blood-curdling? Hope he won't hurt himself."

Thousands of children died along the way. Only a few graves, like Elva's, have any kind of marker.
(Wyoming State Archives)

In most wagons, a loaded rifle hung between the wooden bows of the cover, near the driver's head. That way, a driver could grab it quickly to shoot a buffalo or defend the wagon against Indian attack. Emigrants often accidentally shot themselves or others when they hit the trigger or pulled out their rifles muzzles first. There were probably more deaths from the pioneers' own weapons than from all the combined Indian attacks.

John Minto reported that "I got me a nice new rifle. I also . . . purchased five pounds of powder, twenty-five pounds of lead, one dozen boxes of percussion caps, five pounds of shot, and one gross of fishhooks and lines to match: also I bought two pocket knives, two sheath knives, a hatchet to answer for a tomahawk, and an axe."

Teenager Mary Eliza Warner narrowly missed death from a gun resting against her wagon. When she jumped off the wagon, the gun fired and shot off a lock of her hair. Like Catherine Sager, Mary Eliza was lucky.

One evening, Lucy Ann Henderson's little sister took the medicine bag off the nail and opened it. While her mother was cooking supper, six-year-old Salita swallowed all the laudanum. Within a few hours, she was dead. Lucy Ann recalled that

Many pioneers carried the Sharps' carbine, one of the best-selling rifles of the time. Rifles were used for hunting and protection but were also a major cause of accidental injuries and deaths.

(Kansas State Historical Society)

> Father . . . made a coffin . . . of black walnut boards we used for a table . . . for Salita and we buried her there by the roadside in the desert. . . . Three days after my little sister . . . died we stopped for a few hours, and my sister Olivia was born. . . . The men of the party decided . . . we had to press on. The going was terribly

Worried parents sometimes put small children on a leash or in a box to prevent them from stepping on a rattlesnake, getting lost, or being kidnapped by Indians. These wagons are on the Gila Trail, east of Yuma, Arizona.

rough. The men walked beside the wagons and tried to ease the wheels down into the rough places, but in spite of this it was a very rough ride for my mother and her new born babe. There were five of us children.

It was hard to watch each child all the time, and parents worried constantly. In almost every wagon train, at least one child was run over by a heavy wheel. Other children wandered away. It was easy to get lost on the vast sameness of the prairie while gathering firewood or looking for treasures to collect. Most children stumbled into another wagon train camp or spent a rainy, tearful night under a tree before being rescued. Some were never found. A few were kidnapped by Indians.

Lucy Knight, one of seven children in a family going to Oregon, was accidentally left behind. Her mother wrote on August 8, 1853: "Here we left unknowingly our Lucy behind, not a soul had missed her until we had gone some miles, when we stopped a while to rest the cattle." No one even worried, because Lucy liked to play with friends in other wagons. Another train found the eight-year-old and returned her to her mother. Afterward, Mrs. Knight learned that Lucy "was terribly frightened and so was some more of us, when we found out what a narrow escape she had run. She said she was sitting under the bank of the river when we started, busy watching some wagons cross, and did not know we were ready."

Chapter Ten

INDIANS

Even before leaving home, Jesse Applegate and many other young people believed that "we would have to travel through a country swarming with wild Indians who would try to kill us with tomahawks and scalp us."

Most white people had been brought up at home and taught in school to fear Indians. As they prepared for their trips, families pored over newspaper articles and editorials about Indians attacking wagon trains, kidnapping children, and scalping everyone. These articles were often incorrect or exaggerated. Some women and their daughters read popular captivity novels, usually written by authors who had never been west. One anxious mother cut her daughter's long hair so she wouldn't be scalped.

From grandparents and other relatives, children heard war stories, plus stories of slaughter and captivity, where Indians grabbed babies from their cradles. Virginia Reed's grandmother told her about an aunt who was captured by Indians and escaped five years later. Many of the stories were, as Adrietta Hixon wrote long after she had reached Oregon, "the folklore . . . [of] my childhood."

Still, everyone worried. At the jumping-off points, the men bought extra guns and knives to protect themselves and their families from the "red savages." Family members tried to sort out what was real information, not gossip, pertaining to Indian atrocities on the trail.

As people gathered around the evening campfires on the trail, the stories continued. Marion Russell recalled that Captain Aubry, the leader of her wagon train, told the children to "have eyes in the back of your head, and keep all your eyes open at night and day. [They] will steal the hair from your head if you're not careful."

In general, the emigrants knew very little about the twenty or so tribes they might encounter along the trail. Although some stories were true, most were rumors that had spread as quickly as a prairie wildfire. Early travelers, like Lewis and Clark, found the Indians to be friendly and helpful, as did many later emigrants.

With his mother, four brothers, and a sister, eleven-year-old Elisha Brooks started for California in 1852. Elisha's father was a gold miner there, and the family was going to join him. In Council Bluffs, Iowa, Elisha met his first Indians. "A band of blanketed, feathered, beaded, fringed, wild looking objects barred our way. I slunk under the wagon in abject terror, peering through the wheels," he later recalled. Elisha quickly discovered that

A Plains Indian. The Plains Indian tribes, including the Sioux, Comanche, Blackfoot, Kiowa, Crow, Cheyenne, and Dakota, roamed from the Mississippi River to the Rocky Mountains. They hunted buffalo on horseback, starting in the seventeenth century, after Europeans brought horses to North America.
(DRAWING BY JACK ZANE, USED COURTESY OF HIS FAMILY)

he had overreacted. These Indians were not going to hurt him. Other children were just as fearful as Elisha, but many did not see a single Indian on the way west.

Sometimes emigrants frightened Indians. When Edward Lenox's wagon train turned a bend in 1843 and approached an Indian village:

> Men and squaws and children altogether tore down the wigwams. They ran to their ponies, the squaws lashed the tent poles to them, leaving the ends dragging on the ground. Tepees, buffalo robes, cooking utensils, provisions, and everything . . . was gathered up in an incredible short space of time. . . . They were afraid of our "walking lodges."

This Cheyenne family is preparing to travel to another hunting area using a travois, a sledlike framework of wooden tepee poles. It carries their belongings and small children.
(COFFRIN'S OLD WEST GALLERY, MONT./CHRISTIAN BARTHELMESS)

During the migration years when Edward, Elisha, and Virginia were heading west, North America's native people were struggling to con-

Pawnees followed the buffalo herds, and several generations lived in each hide-covered tepee.
(KANSAS STATE HISTORICAL SOCIETY)

tinue their centuries-old way of life. In the 1830s, Congress had created a huge new "Indian Territory" west of the Missouri River. One by one, eastern tribes were forced to give up their land and move to this area. Some went willingly, but most did not. The Cherokees were driven from their homes, and two thousand died on what is remembered as the Trail of Tears.

Thousands of Indians had been relocated, and now white families were crossing their territory in covered wagons. "The White-Topped Road" alarmed many tribes, but relationships between whites and Indians stayed relatively peaceful in the 1840s. Indians and male emigrants often sat in a circle to smoke a long-stemmed peace pipe. The pipe-smoking ceremony symbolized friendship and was especially meaningful for the Indians when they realized that the emigrants were not settling on their land.

Eliza Ann McAuley went west in 1852, a busy year on the trail, and recorded in her diary that "the Indians are very friendly and visit us often." One night, a Pawnee chief and twelve braves camped near them. Eliza Ann wrote that "at break of day, the Indians awoke us, singing their morning song . . . and it was very harmonious and pleasing."

Sallie Hester felt differently. "We are now in the Pawnee Nation. . . . They never make their appearance during the day, but skulk around at night, steal cattle, and do all the mischief they can." Sallie probably was not aware that Sioux warriors had driven the Pawnees from their

Young pioneers sometimes played with Indian children, like these Crow toddlers.
(AMERICAN HERITAGE CENTER, UNIVERSITY OF WYOMING)

homes and killed many of them. Then the emigrants burned wood, fed grass to their stock, and hunted wild game as they passed through the Pawnee Nation. No wonder that the Pawnees were forced to steal and beg to survive.

After weeks on the trail, most young people began to overcome their terror. Unlike their parents, children were curious and more likely to notice the differences among the tribes. The early part of the trip was a wonderful adventure, and that included meeting Indians of all ages. Jesse Applegate saw some Indian men who "were more than six feet tall, straight, and moved with a proud step; wore blankets drawn around their shoulders and leggins. Their hair was shorn to the scalp, except something like a rooster's comb on top of the head, colored red." Virginia Reed, in a letter home, wrote that the Sioux were the prettiest dressed of all the tribes she had seen.

Young people peered in tepees and wigwams. Sometimes they saw women and children sewing. They smiled at and played with Indian babies and toddlers. Other times, the Indians might be eating grasshoppers or preparing a stew made of dog meat. The different foods they ate were both shocking and exciting.

One girl recalled a group of Snake Indian women, who were camped nearby, watching her mother sew. "They jabbered and laughed. Finally Mother gave one of them a needle and thread, and [the woman] was so pleased, then all of them wanted one."

Indian children, just like the young people on the wagon trains, played games. Relay races, tug of war, and wrestling were popular. Boys, as they grew older, played hunting games with bow and arrows. These games prepared them for lives as warriors. Emigrants watched the warriors race about camp on their horses, showing off their war-making skills. Girls tended to play games revolving around cooking and home life.

Crossing the prairie, some pioneers discovered that many tribes buried their dead in trees or on scaffolding. Rachel Taylor saved a feather that had fallen from a burial site. For other children, it was tempting to peek! After breakfast one morning, Charley True and his dog, Prince, were out walking when he came upon the corpse of an Indian. It was

lying on its back on two poles suspended at each end between two trees. It was about six feet above the ground and completely dried up, till it appeared to be mummified. By its sides were still various articles belonging to him in life, just as they had been left . . . a bow and quiver with arrows, pipe and knives and sheath, and various trinkets dear to every Indian heart.

Some Indian tribes, like these Sioux, frequently buried their dead in trees. This is the body of Chief Spotted Tail's daughter, wrapped tightly in buffalo hides and placed on scaffolding between branches.
(L. Tom Perry Special Collections, Harold B. Lee Library, Brigham Young University/William Henry Jackson)

Pioneers also saw tribes prepare for war against one another and watched war dances before battles. Maria Elliott wrote:

> We met a party of Indian warriors. They were dressed very well; had capes and coats on and a great many ornaments. Some had beads on their necks, brass earrings, and finger rings on every finger. Some had tin ornaments for a sash; the tin was round and about two inches in diameter. They also had feathers on their head. They came up . . . and shook hands with us. Said they were Pawnees.

Lucy Ann Henderson was at Fort Laramie when a group of painted Indians jumped, yelled, and waved their tomahawks around the campfire. The Indians both scared and fascinated her.

Some tribes settled near forts and trading posts, where they could trade for guns, knives, blankets, and other goods. Along with their wagon train, two brothers were camped near Fort Laramie. Sioux tepee villages sat on the surrounding hills. Traders and Indians mingled with the emigrants. "This a.m. the Indians made a visit to our camp, men, women & children. With 5 of the most splendid Banners waving in the [breeze], a present of tobacco, Powder, lead, & other things were made them. Then the men sit down & took a smoke. All out of the same hatchet pipe, in true indian stile." That night, the members of the wagon train tried to sleep to the endless barking of Indian dogs.

Further west, in Soda Springs, Idaho, Eliza Ann McAuley traded with a Shoshone man. She exchanged bread and sugar for a handmade pair of moccasins. During her months on the trail, Eliza Ann grew less shy about learning Indian customs and even spoke some Shoshone words.

Young people enjoyed bartering trinkets with Indian children in exchange for such items as beadwork or clothing. Because of these brief, meaningful meetings, they began to learn about one another's ways.

In Oregon's Blue Mountains, a chief tried to buy John McWilliams as a groom for his daughter. John figured it was because "I had long black hair and no beard, and was sunburned until I was dark as an Indian." The chief called John a "half Indian" and offered him one hundred horses. John said no, "but I never heard the last of it; the boys thought it a good joke on me."

Mary Field, a beautiful redheaded teenager, hid in her family's wagon after an Indian chief offered Mary's mother several ponies for her. Mary wrote that "we were all very worried . . . so Mother decided to hide me [and] took our feather beds and placed them over two boxes and I crawled under there. Sure enough the Indian Chief came back. . . . Mother told him I was lost. . . . [The] chief . . . searched but did not find me. He even felt the feather bed I was under." Mary made it safely to Utah.

Relationships between Indians and emigrants varied. It depended on the year of travel, the place on the trail, and whether or not there had been trouble between a tribe and a wagon train at another time. Fewer than one-tenth of all wagon trains reported any hostile act by Indians. But when problems between Indian tribes and emigrants did occur, it was likely to be during the second half of the trip. This was especially true from the mid-1850s on. In 1850, tens of thousands of pioneers headed west, and the wagon trains stretched as far as the eye could see. Trees and grass disappeared; water holes were polluted. The buffalo were being slaughtered, and the Indians were losing a steady supply of food.

Small bands of angry young warriors fought back, mostly by trying to scare the emigrants away. One pioneer who went hunting was surrounded by a group of Pawnees. After shaking hands with him, they took his clothes and gun. He walked back to his wagon, naked but alive.

Before sunup on the prairie one morning, Mary Ackley recalled, her camp was stirring. She and her father thought they heard birds flying

PHOTOGRAPHING THE WEST

Taking pictures of Indians, pioneers, scenery, and the changing West was hard work in the mid-1850s. Photographers needed about three hundred pounds of equipment. In addition to their big and bulky cameras, they required chemicals, glass plates, tripods, and a light-proof tent. Cameras exposed images on wet-glass plates, and these plates had to be kept moist until developed. These glass plates came in several sizes, some as large as eleven by fourteen inches.

Some photographers packed their gear on mules and prayed that their animals wouldn't buck or fall off a cliff, breaking all the glass plates. Others traveled in wagons they had converted into portable photography studios.

To get the perfect picture, a photographer couldn't just point and shoot. He or she might have to drop into a canyon or race up a mountainside to set up his camera on the tripod. Back he scrambled to get the wet plate, which he kept wrapped in a damp cloth. The photographer took the exposure, or picture, then dashed into his darkroom tent to develop it. This could take forty-five minutes . . . or much longer.

Photographers were happy to have five new pictures in a day. Back home, their black-and-white photographs were popular in newspapers and magazines. Seeing the photographs helped congressmen make decisions about the land and the native people beyond the frontier. William Henry Jackson's photographs of the Yellowstone area helped convince Congress to create Yellowstone National Park in 1872, the country's first national park.

Chief Washakie and other members of his Shoshone tribe pose for photographer William Henry Jackson near South Pass in the Rocky Mountains. (Smithsonian Institution)

overhead in the darkness. "Day was breaking and we were ready to start, when to our surprise and horror we found arrows all over the camp." The "birds" Mary and her father had heard were Indian arrows. "Some had gone through the covers of two wagons, but no one was injured. Several cattle had been killed."

Wagon trains occasionally passed a burned-out cabin or a wagon that had been attacked. One pioneer found a marked grave that said that the dead man had been killed by an Indian arrow. And the actual arrow was sticking out of the grave.

Ten-year-old Jasper Lawn was hitching up his team when an arrow whizzed by and killed Old Buck, one of his oxen. An Indian stood on a hillside. Jasper yelled to his uncle to "kill that Indian," and he did. Fearing retaliation, the wagon train hurried on. When Jasper wrote his memoirs fifty years later, he still spoke negatively about Indians.

On a few occasions children, usually females, were kidnapped along the trail or snatched from frontier cabins. Captured girls and young women became slaves or were bartered to another tribe. Or they were returned in exchange for clothes, guns, and horses. A few girls married Indians and had children before being rescued. Many found it hard to return to regular life. Some preferred Indian life, and others did not easily readjust to the white world. They were often thought of as celebrities, and everyone wanted accounts of their experiences with the "red savages."

There were plenty of emigrants of all ages who believed that Indians were not human beings and that it was okay to hurt or kill them. One of the sons of guide Caleb Greenwood murdered an Indian just for frightening his horse. And he boasted about what he had done.

Indians sometimes scared emigrants into giving them food and horses. They stole horses or scattered the stock. Marion Russell heard war whoops in the night. Other children, as they slept beneath the wagon, had nightmares about being scalped.

Maggie Hall's family was camped on the Rio Grande, en route to southern California. An Apache came into camp one night and took clothing as well as a pony. He "rode away with Mother's dress on," Maggie said.

Children, as well as adults, may not have understood how important horses and other livestock were to the Indians. With new horses, the tribe acquired more wealth and trading ability. And when a warrior stole a horse, he gained status in his tribe.

During the migration years, Indians continued to be curious about the white travelers. Small bands would descend on a wagon train to check out each wagon. Some families welcomed them, shared their food, and gave the Indians simple gifts. Other emigrants were not friendly and chased them off with gunfire or told the Indians, often falsely, that they had deadly smallpox.

The symbols that decorate this Assiniboine tepee on the northern plains were an important part of the Indian tribe's religious beliefs and ceremonies.

One teenage emigrant recalled that his Indian visitors climbed into wagons, touched things, and dipped their fingers in kettles to taste the food. They camped nearby and listened to violin music each night. The Indians were fascinated by the white-skinned travelers, especially the blond-haired children and the bearded men. Even the handcarts many Mormons pushed west intrigued the Indians, and they called them "little wagons."

At times, the Indians were more than curious. Sarah Yorke recalled an incident at their campsite when a group of Indians came to claim a horse that they believed belonged to them. Sarah wrote that

> we could see the Indians coming from every direction, all painted up, with their feathers—all ready for war. My older brother, Dick, was on [the horse] and the Indians just walked up and took hold of the bridle and started to lead the horse away with my brother on and my father had to lift my brother off the horse and let the Indians take it. It was the only thing he could do—we didn't dare do anything else.

To make sure they had a safe journey, Mormon leader Brigham Young asked his people to treat all Indians with kindness. They were to feed them, not fight them. The Mormons had fewer Indian problems than the other white emigrants.

Children wrote in journals and letters about villages they passed on the way west. They were all different, from the hide-covered tepees of the Sioux, who followed the buffalo, to the more permanent dome-shaped earth lodges of the Pawnees. Children described the Indians they saw, including some who came into their camps. The daughter of a Sioux chief visited ten-year-old Kate McDaniel's wagon train.

> [She] was about fifteen years old and . . . very beautiful. . . . She was dressed in a loose white buckskin gown, soft as silk. . . . The

skirt came to her knees and she wore long leggings. The bottom of the dress had deep fringes on it. . . . The little princess, as we like to call her, let us pet her pony and then she showed us she could ride and what her pony could do. . . . Then [she] jumped into her saddle, waved her hand to us, and with a little giggling laugh, was gone like a beautiful bird.

Indians generally wanted blankets, firearms, and tobacco. They might trade moccasins and meat for beads, buttons, and mirrors. Since many of the emigrants did not have time to hunt, they were happy to buy fresh buffalo or salmon. Indians also sold the pioneers sturdy

This Kiowa girl, dressed in the fringed clothing typical of her tribe, sits on her beautiful pony.
(MISSOURI HISTORICAL SOCIETY)

horses to replace their weakened or lost animals. Other tribes learned to charge the emigrants for helping them over rivers or guiding them across a difficult stretch of land. Indians often generously shared information about the trail ahead.

Elisha Brooks, age eleven, wrote that after their driver deserted them, a band of Crow Indians camped with his family for a week.

> We presented a strange and weird scene . . . red men in rich robes of bear and panther skins decked out with fringe and feathers, red men without robes or feathers, and unwashed; favorite and actually handsome squaws in elegant mantles of bird skins, tattooed and adorned with beads; unlovely squaws in scanty rags and no beads, and unwashed; papooses in . . . cradles grinning . . . ; ponies hidden under monumental burdens; packs of dogs creeping under wonderful loads, and bringing up the rear an old ox team with six wild, ragged children and a woman once called white and sometimes unwashed, for we could not always get water enough to drink. We were a Wild West Show.

Relationships between white travelers and Indians deteriorated further when during the later years of the covered wagon migration, the United States government stepped in to protect the travelers from increasingly frequent Indian attacks. They purchased and improved forts or built new ones between the Missouri River and the Pacific Ocean, and blue-coated soldiers moved into Fort Kearny, Fort Laramie, Fort Caspar, Fort Bridger, and Fort Hall. Following the end of the Civil War in 1865, the government sent more soldiers west.

This buildup of soldiers further upset the Indians, and battles between the two groups became more common. The United States government, local settlers, and military commanders often broke treaties they had made with various Indian tribes. It usually happened after gold or other precious metals were discovered. At the start of a gold rush in the Black Hills of South Dakota in 1874, land that had been promised to local Indians suddenly became valuable. Greedy prospectors and settlers ignored the existing treaties between the Indians and the United States government. And the Indians were blamed for trying to defend their property.

There was a long period of wars with bloody battles in Montana like Custer's Last Stand and the Sand Creek Massacre in Colorado Territory. Since single wagons or small groups were more likely to be targets, wagon trains drew together so that they would be harder to attack.

Harriet Hitchcock put in her journal that "the Indians are murdering the whites on the plains at a rapid rate." But soldiers were murdering Indian men, women, and children, too. After learning about the 1864 Sand Creek Massacre, Harriet wrote that soldiers

> destroyed a village of 1000 Cheyennes. The next day while the soldiers were burning the wigwams three little Indian children were found hidden under some Buffalo robes. They were nearly frightened to death. The soldiers brought them here. . . . Bell [her sister] has made a dress for the little girl and I have made her an apron. She is very shy and afraid of white people.

By the time pioneers reached California, they had often met many Indian tribes. The Miwok, Maidu, Pomo, and Yurok tended to gather and hunt food, not farm, and relied on acorns, small game, and fish. This Indian, Alice Frank, is from the Yurok tribe.
(DRAWING BY JACK ZANE, USED COURTESY OF HIS FAMILY)

The orphaned Indian children were sent back east to be educated, Harriet added. The Sand Creek Massacre was one of the worst Indian slaughters in the history of Indian-settler relations. American soldiers from the Colorado Cavalry killed hundreds of Indians, then scalped the dead and mutilated the bodies.

For some tribes, fighting back was often the only way to protect what they knew. They couldn't be silent and watch white settlers kill buffalo and cross their ancestral homelands. Warriors formed war parties; soldiers patrolled the trails. But for the Indians, there were too many forts and soldiers along the roads west. White settlers took more and more Indian land, forcing them onto reservations—land that no one wanted because the soil was so poor. Tribes were losing their ancestral lands to ranchers, railroad companies, and homesteaders.

Red Cloud, Chief of the Oglala Sioux, worked hard to save his people and homeland above the North Platte River. In 1870, he traveled to Washington, D.C., to meet with President Ulysses S. Grant. "I have come here to tell the Great White Father what I do not like about this country. White people have surrounded me and have left me nothing but an island. When we first had this land we were strong. Now we are melting like snow on the hillside, while you are growing like spring grass."

This was happening to Indian tribes across the country, but no one

This chief is forbidding travel over his territory. The scout might first try to trade some blankets, beads, or food for permission to cross the land; otherwise he will have to find a new trail.

expressed it as eloquently as Chief Red Cloud. The truth was that most whites still believed that Indians were savages and that the land was not theirs.

Marion Russell remembered the various tribes "who watched with bitter eyes that vast migration." The Indian way of life was being destroyed and everyone—Indians and whites—knew it.

Chapter Eleven

MOTHER NATURE RULES

For nearly two thousand miles, the pioneers were at the mercy of rapidly changing conditions: wind, rain, lightning, hail, dust, snow, heat, and temperatures that could fall below zero. Their only shelter was a covered wagon or a tent.

Seven-year-old Marion Russell didn't mind. She especially loved the ever-changing sky. "Morning after morning we watched the great land flare into beauty. Evening after evening we watched the prairie sun go down in its glory, and then watched the white stars shine in the night above us. There were also the rainbows . . . that spanned the old trail."

A few days after the Fourth of July, Eugenia Zieber wrote in her journal: "A most lovely evening. The moon is shining brightly, and it is quite calm. One dislikes to close her eyes upon such an evening. Gladly would I sit and think over scenes and pleasures past & gone: but rest is needed."

But the weather was often far from perfect. Powerful rainstorms were common. Kate McDaniel was asleep when one storm struck. She recalled that "we children were quaking in our bed. At each crack of

A prairie storm, sketched by J. G. Bruff in 1849.
(THE HUNTINGTON LIBRARY)

thunder, which we thought would crash the top of the wagon down upon us, we would duck our heads under the pillows and draw the covers tightly over us."

Benjamin Bonney wrote in his memoirs about another spectacular night storm when he was seven and his family was camped on the Nebraska prairie.

> The thunder seemed almost incessant, and the lightning was so brilliant, you read by its flashes. . . . Our tents were blown down as were the covers of our prairie schooners and in less than five minutes we were wet as drowned rats. Unless you have been through it, you have no idea of the confusion resulting from a storm on the plains, with the oxen bellowing, the children crying and the men shouting . . . with everything as light as day and the next second as black as the depth of a pit.

When hailstones fell from the sky, the frozen ice balls cut lips and cheeks. Some wagon covers and tents ripped and shredded. Frightened animals bucked and threatened to stampede. While wearing cooking pots for protection, children helped tie down the animals, and then they dove under the wagon beds to wait for the storm to end. Eleven-year-old Elisha Perkins wrote, "Hail exceeded anything I ever saw, being as large as pigeon eggs. . . . There may be fun in camping, but we haven't discovered any."

Catherine Sager and her family went west in 1844, and nonstop rains tore at the canvas wagon top and battered their oxen. Huddled inside the wagon with her little sisters, Catherine listened to the sucking sound the wheels made in the hub-deep mud.

If wagons became stuck, families waited for the storm to pass. Then children helped gather long grasses to lay on the ground in front of the wheels. Oxen pulled the wagon from the front, and people pushed from behind. Slowly the wheels rolled out of the mud onto the grass.

Heavy rains could cause rivers to become too full or dangerous to cross. Once, Catherine Sager recalled in her memoirs, during another storm, "the river near which we encamped rose and overflowed its bank, until we had to move back nearly a day's journey. Water ran through the tent, and the bedclothes were saturated."

It was common to wait three or four days for a river to go down and be safe enough to ford. Wagon train captains, with the aid of their scouts, rode along the bank to find the best place to cross.

Before fording a river, each wagon bed had to be waterproofed. Children filled cracks with tar or candle wax mixed with ashes. Then several teams of animals were hooked to the wagon to make sure it got safely across. The animals might have to pull a wagon through quicksand before it got stuck or tipped over. With as many as fifty wagons in a train, it could take several days to get everyone to the other side of a big river. Jesse Applegate recalled when his family forded the South Fork of the Platte River:

Mother, myself, and the other children were in the . . . wagon. . . .
As we were just getting up the bank from the ford, our team broke
loose and wagon and team backed into the river. Being swept
below the ford, the team swam and the wagon sank down and was
drifting on the sand; and I remember the water came rushing into
the wagon box to my waist, compelling me to scramble up on the
top of a trunk. . . . But several men came swimming, held up the
wagon, and soon assisted us to shore.

In this 1850 photograph, families are fording what is possibly the Big Blue River in Kansas, a dangerous and difficult task. Note the horses swimming beside the wagons.
(Nebraska State Historical Society)

Deeper rivers had to be ferried. At some rivers, flat ferryboats carried
entire wagons, families, and stock to the other side for a fee. Mormon
leader Brigham Young established a ferry for his people and other emigrants near Fort Caspar on the North Platte River.

Pioneers sometimes prepared the wagon box so they could more easily float it across the river like a boat. They pulled off the canvas top and stored it and the wheels in the wagon bed. Then they water-proofed the bed or tacked buffalo skins over the bottom. Children and women huddled inside, and one or two men joined them, steering the wagon with long poles. Horseback riders swam beside the wagon, helping from the outside. It was dangerous in the fast currents. Animals and people drowned during some of these crossings. On the far shore, the wagon was put together again.

During rainstorms, rivers turned muddy. Some, like the Platte River, were always murky-looking. Helen Carpenter noted that "the water is full of yellow sediment and looks still thicker and less inviting than

The toll for a wagon and two animals might have been twenty cents on this rope ferry across the Kansas River.

THE PLATTE RIVER

The Platte River angles westward from the Missouri River. Some say that the river was first known as Nebrathka, an Indian word for weeping water. Long ago, buffalo and Indian trails followed its banks. Then came the trappers, on foot, on horseback, or leading pack trains of mules loaded down with furs. French trappers named the flat, wide river the Platte, and the name stuck.

Except for islands covered with willows and cottonwoods, the river offered pioneers little shade, and its water was poor-tasting. The Platte was too shallow to be ferried and dangerous to ford. Quicksand lined the bottom in spots and slowly sucked at toes, boots, hooves, and wagon wheels. Thick with swirling sand and debris, the fast-moving river swallowed children if they tumbled from wagons and swept away stock.

Oregon- and California-bound emigrants followed the Platte River on the south side. They camped near Chimney Rock, a five-hundred-foot-high clay-and-sandstone tower along the river, their first major landmark. Farther on, they rested and bought supplies at Fort Laramie. The Mormon Trail took the north bank road.

The Platte River led everyone west toward South Pass in the Rocky Mountains.

Missouri River water." Children hauled water to camp and had to wait several hours for the silt to settle at the bottom of the bucket and the water to become usable.

Helen had been on the road about a month when she wrote: "The heat has been intolerable, the bright sunshine on the white wagon covers has been blinding, the dust suffocating, and the mosquitoes painfully tormenting. Mosquitoes all day long and they are here for the night and we have nothing to protect ourselves in any way."

With warm weather, especially along the rivers, mosquitoes were a big problem. One mother wrote, "Muskitoes almost eat me up. The children look like they had the measles." When the mosquitoes were troublesome, children would light a dry buffalo chip and place it

Settlers hurried wagons across the shallower streams and rivers, hoping to avoid getting trapped in quicksand.
(THE HUNTINGTON LIBRARY/
FREDERICK MONSEN)

inside the wagon. This soon smoked out the tiny insects, but it probably didn't smell very good.

Besides mosquitoes, Helen and other emigrants battled buffalo gnats. They swarmed around, getting into eyes, noses, and mouths. June bugs crawled over everything, so numerous they could be picked up by the handful.

Warm weather could suddenly shift and turn cold. Swift storms blew across the prairie. Most of the time, Helen stayed cheerful, but one time, she wrote about a windstorm that struck while she and her aunt were sleeping.

I am wondering just how hard the wind has to blow before it is called a tornado. The wagon was so shaken up that one could not tell which way the vibrations were, backward, forward, side-wise, or all three together. Aunt Sis was curious and putting her head outside came near going overboard and lost a fine new silk handkerchief that was doing duty as a night cap.

Clouds of dust circled the moving wagon trains. Everyone and everything became covered in dirt. Eliza Ann McAuley, who was going to California's gold fields, wrote about a day in July when it was "so windy and dusty . . . that sometimes we could scarcely see the length of the team." That night the wind was still blowing. She wrote by candlelight that "we cannot see the tent or get any supper, so we take a cold bite and go to bed in the wagon."

Dust filtered through the canvas covers, and it covered everything—clothes, food, bedding, and people. Travelers washed out their eyes with cool water and kept a handkerchief around their mouths and

Unexpected blizzards swept over the prairie, and occasional summer snow fell in the mountains. Weakened oxen and other animals often died.

noses. As one pioneer wrote, "How can I give you any idea of it? We are almost blinded by it. My eyes are very sore. It tries my patience more than anything else."

As more and more people took to the trail, they had a hard time finding fresh drinking water. Streams and springs became polluted. They smelled terrible. Thick green scum floated on top of the often warm water. Thousands of wiggling mosquito larvae fed on the green algae. Some ponds and springs had too much salt, or alkalinity, which could poison people and animals.

Sometimes the thirsty animals tried to drink the water anyway. Eliza Ann wrote that she "had to cross a very bad alkali swamp and had to rush the cattle through to keep them from drinking the water. When they get alkalied the remedy is a good dose of whiskey."

Eliza Ann and the other pioneers had to act quickly so their animals

Vicious windstorms sometimes struck the prairie.
(Missouri Historical Society)

wouldn't die. They treated any animals that lagged behind, seemed unusually tired, or began to vomit. "Bacon and grease were the only antidotes for poison that our stores contained," wrote one pioneer, "so we cut slices of bacon and forced it down the throats of the sick oxen, who after once tasting the bacon ate it eagerly, thereby saving their lives."

Everyone on the trail, including children, learned to drink coffee, since it disguised the water's bad taste and killed any bugs in the water. And in one journal, the writer joked that even his horse preferred coffee to water.

A driver cracks a bull whip over thirsty oxen to hurry them past a poisonous water hole.
(COLORADO HISTORICAL SOCIETY)

Chapter Twelve

DRY AND HOT

There are four desert areas in the American West, and the pioneers had to cross at least one, depending on the route. To learn more about the deserts, travelers often studied guidebooks like Randolph Marcy's *The Prairie Traveler*. After months of travel, most families were tired of the long, hard journey. They were scared, too, of the desert. There weren't many water holes in the desert, and daytime temperatures could soar to over 100 degrees.

The Santa Fe Trail and the Gila Trail angled southwest through seemingly endless desert stretches that could be dry, barren, and hot. While parents worried, children spotted scorpions, sidewinders, tarantulas, and other desert animals. Marion Russell wrote in her memoirs, "Sometimes little jeweled lizards would dart across our path, to stop, panting, in the shade of a scanty bush. Birds with long tails would walk the trail before us. . . . The drivers called them road-runners."

Part of the California Trail lay between the Rocky Mountains and the Sierra Nevada, in the desertlike region now called the Great Basin. California-bound travelers followed a dusty trail near the Humboldt

River for hundreds of miles. The most dreaded section was the Forty Mile Desert, a waterless wasteland that started a few miles beyond the Humboldt Sink, where the river ended. By then, animals and people were worn out.

If they could find it, the men cut grass for the stock and stored it inside the wagons before tackling the Forty Mile Desert. But in Lucy Ann Henderson's wagon train, there was no grass or grain for the cattle. "Mother," she wrote, "baked up a lot of bread to feed them."

Women and children filled every water container they had, including coffeepots and boots. The men lashed forty-gallon water barrels to the sides of the wagon. Pioneers called them "ox breakers" because they were so heavy and hard on the animals.

It was slow going in the hills, so this large wagon train on the Santa Fe Trail may have divided to get to the flatlands more quickly.
(Denver Public Library, Western History Collection)

On any of the desert routes, the train's captain might order everyone to travel on until midnight to reach a water hole or go by moonlight to avoid the hot sun. Even at night, warm, dry desert winds blew endlessly, drying out the eyes and throats of people and animals. It was hard to avoid thorny cactus plants in the faint light or to know the location of a buzzing rattlesnake.

Fathers and sons walked beside their tired oxen, watching in the darkness for the dim outlines of their heads and horns to see if they were beginning to droop. Everyone—children, women, and men—looked ragged and dirty. There just wasn't enough time to worry about personal appearance.

Emigrants taking the Oregon Trail passed over dry desert lands before they reached the Blue Mountains. But the crossing wasn't as difficult as on other trails. Benjamin Bonney wrote about seeing strange-

Alexander Gardner, a well-known photographer, took this desert scene along a southwestern trail in 1867.
(MISSOURI HISTORICAL SOCIETY)

looking cactus and thin-bladed yucca plants a few weeks after his family pulled out of its Oregon-bound train at Fort Hall and headed southwest toward California.

> We struck a desert of sand and sage brush. On this sage brush plain we found lots of prickly pears [a kind of cactus]. We children were bare-footed and I can remember yet how we limped across the desert, for we cut the soles of our feet on the prickly pears. . . . They also made the oxen lame, for the spines would work in between the oxen's hoofs.

The wagons rolled past more and more sagebrush, some as tall as a child and tough enough to overturn a light wagon. Without wood or buffalo chips for fuel, children whacked off branches and carried armfuls back to camp. The sagebrush made a hot, bright fire for roasting rabbits and sage hens, a type of grouse—if they were lucky enough to shoot any. After supper, boys carefully checked each water barrel for leaks. It was their job to seal the cracks with tar.

Later travelers began to leave signs at some of the water holes along the various routes. "Look at this—look at this! The water here is poison, and we have lost six of our cattle. Do not let your cattle drink on this bottom," read one such message.

Out of desperation, some emigrants dug pits to try and find more water, even if it was muddy. But the smell of water drove thirsty cattle crazy. They raced to the pits and fell in headfirst and drowned. The pits became choked with bloated carcasses. Only the hindquarters and tails of the animals poked out of the holes. This caused a terrible smell and quickly spoiled the water for other wagon trains.

Dry salt beds covered parts of the desert. Oxen and wagon wheels stirred up alkali dust. The fine white powder stung eyes and throats. Sallie Hester noted on August 18, 1849, that the "roads are . . . trying to our wagons . . . grass has been scarce . . . the water is not fit to drink—slough water—we are obliged to use it, for it's all we have." The family was taking the Sublette Cutoff and coming up on the Humboldt River, according to Sallie's journal.

Everyone's hands and faces were chapped. Charley True complained that "the alkaline dust and water acted like a solution [that burned], and the slightest friction caused the blood to flow from the cracks of our faces and hands."

There were also springs in the desert. Some spurted high like geysers; others gurgled and steamed. Some, bringing up sulfurous minerals from deep underground, stank of rotten eggs. Sixteen-year-old Eliza Ann McAuley wrote in her diary on September 4: "These springs boil up with great noise, emitting a very nauseous smell. . . . We hear that a woman and child have got scalded very badly by stepping into one of them." Like the Hesters, the McAuley group crossed the desert near the Humboldt River.

Oxen went lame. Some pioneers made booties for their animals or smeared tar and grease on their hooves to keep the sand and cactus from hurting them even more.

Violent summer cloudbursts struck the desert with little warning.

After their animals died, these pioneers had to move essential items, like food, tools, and seeds, into other wagons and abandon everything else.
(Library of Congress)

The salty crust on top of the soil turned into mushy mud. Animals and wagons sank in the mire. Exhausted oxen had to be cut loose from the wagons to fend for themselves. Many had to be shot. Hungry pioneers might pause briefly to start a fire with wooden wheels and other wagon parts. Before going on, the pioneers fried steaks and liver from their dead oxen.

Without enough animals to pull the heavy wagons, people lightened their loads. Furniture, clothes, and dishes littered the desert. Pioneers passed the stinking, decaying bodies of horses, oxen, and mules. They saw graves of men, women, and children who had died during earlier crossings. And unseen coyotes yipped and yowled all night long. John Brier, who was six, thought he would die in the desert and never see California. The family was on the Old Spanish Trail through the Southwest in 1849, but his father took a cutoff, hoping to save several weeks of travel time. John later recalled:

> We had been without water for twenty-four hours, when sud-
> denly there broke into view to the south a splendid sheet of
> water, which all of us believed was Owen's Lake. As we hur-
> ried towards it, the vision faded, and near midnight we halted
> on the rim of a basin of mud, with a shallow pool of brine.
> From this point on I remember little of our westward course
> across the great desert.

For six weeks, the Brier family had little water or food. They abandoned their wagons, loading what they could directly onto the oxen. John and his four-year-old brother pleaded with their mother for water, but there was never enough. They staggered on. Wind and sand blasted them as they crossed what is now called Death Valley in the Mojave Desert. John and his brother could barely talk because their parched lips and tongues were so swollen.

On February 4, 1850, the Brier Party was rescued. John and his fam-

Juliet and James Brier in 1852. Their children are Columbus (on the left) *and John, with Kirk in front.*
(CHRIS BREWER, BEAR STATE BOOKS)

ily were taken to a ranch and treated to a grand feast. They rested for several days before going on to Los Angeles.

Susan Thompson and her family traveled from Iowa across the southwestern deserts. At first, she wrote that "we were a happy, carefree lot of young people and the dangers and hardships found no resting place on our shoulders. It was a continuous picnic." Susan, who was nearly eighteen, played her violin around the evening campfire and "played games or told stories or danced."

But before long, the dust and heat were daily challenges. As they traveled through Comanche, then Apache country in the Sonoran Desert, Susan wrote about Indians who stole their horses and mules. Food supplies were low. And there were stories circulating of Apaches and Comanches who kidnapped settlers to use as slaves or as barter with other Indians.

Frightened and no longer carefree, Susan recorded: "From here to Tucson, Arizona, we suffered for bread. The [captain] allowed each person but a biscuit and a half per day. We tried to eat hawks and I recall how sick my mother was when she attempted to drink some soup made from coyote meat."

There were seven families in the train, including the Oatmans and the Thompsons. Some families, when they reached Tucson, stopped for several weeks. Animals and people needed to recover. The Oatmans, with their seven children, pushed on. As twelve-year-old Olive recalled, "With scanty supplies, a long journey and hostile Indians to contend with [my father] resolved to proceed under the protection of God, trusting he might reach Fort Yuma in safety."

Susan Thompson later learned from Lorenzo, Olive's oldest brother, that the family was attacked by Apaches a few days later. Although badly wounded, Lorenzo escaped. He walked back down the trail for three days until he found help. Rescuers found the bodies of his parents and siblings, except for Olive's and Mary Ann's. It was too rocky to dig a grave, so they covered the mutilated bodies with rocks. At first, no one was sure what had happened to the two girls. Later they learned they had been kidnapped.

Susan and her family joined a large group for safety, and they made their way from Tucson to Fort Yuma. Susan wrote that "we . . . passed the graves of our friends . . . [and] cast one horrified glance at the pitiful pile of rocks and what they all too plainly disclosed." They finally reached southern California. It would be many years before Susan was reunited with her friend Olive.

THE KIDNAPPING OF OLIVE OATMAN

In 1851, twelve-year-old Olive Oatman started west with her family and some neighbors. They planned to settle on the lower Colorado River in what is now Arizona. The desert was hot, dry, and dangerous. Apaches were on the warpath.

By mid-March, the Oatman family was alone. Everyone else was afraid of the Apaches. The lone wagon rattled toward Fort Yuma, 150 miles away on the Colorado River. The family reached the Gila River at dusk and prepared to camp. A band of Apaches attacked them. Olive and her little sister, Mary Ann, were taken prisoners.

Olive and Mary Ann became slaves. A year later, the Apaches traded them to the Mohave Indians. Each girl was tattooed, with five vertical tribal marks, from chin to lower lip. With the women of the tribe, the sisters dug up edible roots, pounded seeds into mush, gathered wood, and hauled water. It was a hard, harsh life, and the girls, as well as the Indians, were often hungry.

Five years after being kidnapped, Olive was ransomed and returned to the white world at Fort Yuma. Mary Ann had died earlier, probably from starvation. It was at Fort Yuma where Olive first learned that their older brother, Lorenzo, had survived the attack. Everyone else had died.

Olive never forgot her captors, especially some of the Mohave women who became her friends. Topeka, the daughter of the chief, had been as close to her as a sister. Olive wrote and spoke about her captivity, often with respect for some of the Indian ways. She later married John B. Fairchild, and they lived in Texas until her death in 1903.

Olive Oatman still had the tattoos made by her Mohave Indian captors when this picture was taken. (ARIZONA HISTORICAL SOCIETY)

Sallie Hester, who was farther north, wrote in her diary on September 4, 1849:

> Had a trying time crossing [the desert]. Several of our cattle gave out and we left one. The weary journey last night, the mooing of the cattle for water, their exhausted condition, with the cry of "Another ox down," the stopping of the train to unyoke the poor dying brute, to let him follow at will or stop by the wayside and die, and the weary, weary tramp of men and beasts worn out with heat and famished for water, will never be erased from my memory. Just at dawn, in the distance, we had a glimpse of Truckee River, and with it the feeling: Saved at last! Poor cattle; they kept on mooing, even when they stood knee deep in water. The long dreaded desert had been crossed.

The Brooks family crossed the same desert in 1852. They had eaten the last of their flapjacks and bacon. Elisha tried to encourage Old

The Ruby Rivera family crosses a hot, dry stretch of sagebrush.
(DENVER PUBLIC LIBRARY, WESTERN HISTORY DEPARTMENT)

Brock and Nig, the only two oxen they had left, to pull the wagon. Ahead, he saw a man on a mule. "He rode up and presently with a joyful cry we were in the arms of our father. . . . I have no words to tell you of our surprise and happiness at this meeting. . . . The rainbow of hope grew very large . . . and we could smile again."

The letter Elisha's mother had sent west to her husband, who was working in the California mines, took over three months to reach him. Upon reading the letter, Mr. Brooks had ridden three hundred miles east from the Sacramento Valley, alone on his mule, to find his family.

Elisha knew "that our travels were nearly ended and that a grave in the wilderness or our bones whitening on the desert sands were no longer among the probabilities."

Chapter Thirteen

OVER MOUNTAINS

Besides deserts, travelers had to cross several mountain ranges, depending on the route they took. Many pioneers, flatlanders from Missouri and other midwestern areas, feared the unfamiliar mountains. They learned from guides and guidebooks that it could be freezing cold at the higher elevations, especially at night. If they crossed too late in the year, people, animals, and wagons might get trapped in heavy winter snows.

After three to four months of daily use, wagons were in poor condition. And so were the oxen. Some pioneers rebuilt their wagons into small carts, and once again, heavy items, like washtubs and extra cooking utensils, were thrown out.

For seven-year-old Jesse Applegate, suddenly the trek to Oregon wasn't much fun. While crossing the mountains, Jesse wrote that "we were overtaken by a snowstorm. . . . I remember wading through mud and snow and suffering from the cold and wet."

Catherine Sager and her brother, Francis, were trying to care for their younger brother and sisters. Their parents had died earlier on the trail. Catherine recalled that in the Blue Mountains:

cattle were giving out and left lying in the road. We made but a few miles a day. One day when we were making a fire of wet wood Francis thought to help the matter by holding his powder-horn over a small blaze. Of course the powder-horn exploded. . . . He ran to a creek near by and bathed his hands and face, and came back [without eyelashes] and eyebrows, and his face was blackened beyond recognition.

Some pioneers, including Nancy Kelsey, headed west to California without knowing much about the route. She and her husband started for California in May of 1841.

After crossing South Pass in the Rocky Mountains, Nancy recalled: "We left our wagons this side of Salt Lake [Utah] and finished our journey on horseback and drove our cattle. I carried my baby [Ann] in front of me on the horse." A few weeks later, when they reached the mountains in California, she said in her memoirs:

> We were then out of provisions, having killed and eaten all our cattle. I walked barefeeted until my feet were blistered and lived on roasted acorns for two days. . . . My husband came very near dying with cramps, and it was suggested to leave him, but I said I would never do that, and we ate a horse and remained over till the next day, when he was able to travel.

By mid-October, snow covered the mountains. Nancy wrote: "We crossed the Sierra Nevada . . . [and] camped on the summit [of Sonora Pass, which is nearly ten thousand feet high]. It was my eighteenth birthday." After traveling two thousand miles, Nancy and her family finally reached Sutter's Fort on Christmas Day.

Even without snow, it was hard going, especially in the jagged Sierra Nevada. Sometimes the men spent days building a "road bridge." They rolled stones and shoveled dirt to make steep, narrow lanes that would go from one level spot to the next, taking the oxen and the empty wagons up the mountainside. Sarah Ide remembered:

> It took us a long time to go about two miles over our . . . new road up the mountain, over the rough rocks, in some places, and so smooth in others, that the oxen would slip and fall on their knees; the blood from their feet and knees staining the rocks they passed over. It was a trying time—the men swearing at their teams, and beating them most cruelly, all along the rugged way.

In other places, it was impossible to get through. Rock walls and piles of gigantic boulders blocked the route. Emptied wagons had to be hoisted up and over rocky cliff faces by chains and pulleys and ropes and winches. If a chain snapped, a wagon hurtled down a mountain

THE WHITMAN MASSACRE

The seven orphaned Sager children reached the Whitman Mission in October of 1844. Catherine Sager recalled that Narcissa Whitman "had on a dark calico dress and gingham sunbonnet and we thought as we shyly looked at her that she was the prettiest woman we had ever seen."

For the next three years, they lived with Narcissa and Marcus Whitman, along with other children, including the daughter of mountain man Joe Meek. The Whitmans, their adopted parents, were extremely strict but loving. The children attended school, had intensive religious training, and did farm and household chores.

The Whitman Mission was busy. People stopped by: traders, mountain men, and emigrants heading to Oregon. In 1847, several thousand travelers followed the Oregon Trail. Some wagon trains brought measles to the mission. The Indians had little resistance to the disease. About one-half of the local Cayuse tribe died from measles that year, including many of their children. And the leaders blamed Marcus Whitman.

They attacked the mission on November 29, 1847, killing both Whitmans and eleven others, including Francis and John Sager. One Sager sister died from measles a few days after the attack.

Several Cayuse were hanged for their part in the attack. The surviving four Sager sisters each went to separate homes. By the end of 1848, the Whitman Mission was deserted.

and smashed into pieces. The pioneers packed their belongings on the animals and followed a narrow trail through the rocks.

It was just as difficult to go down. Long before the first mountain crossing, families were already leaving cook stoves, trunks, and other heavy items at the side of the trail. To get to the bottom of one hill, Lizzie Charlton wrote in her diary, her brothers and father "had to unhitch & run the waggons down by hand it was so steep."

Moses Schallenberger's wagon train, the Stevens-Murphy Party, reached the Sierra Nevada as the first snows were falling in late 1844.

The emigrants searched frantically for a pass through the mountains. The leaders decided to abandon most of their wagons near a mountain lake. Moses, a tall, thin seventeen-year-old, started to build a twelve-by-fourteen-foot log cabin to protect the pioneers' valuable goods. The rest of the wagons were unloaded and hauled up over a thousand feet of granite rock. Most of the group went ahead on foot or horseback into California.

After completing the cabin, Moses and two other young men set out on snowshoes to catch up with everyone. It was early December, and the snow was already ten feet deep. During the walk, Moses was stricken with leg cramps. Some were so bad that he fell in the snow and cried out in pain. Because he could not keep up with the others, he turned around.

"The feeling of loneliness that came over me," he wrote in his mem-

By 1866, when this picture was taken, there was a road to follow through the mountains. For earlier travelers like Jesse Applegate and Nancy Kelsey, it was rough going.
(LIBRARY OF CONGRESS)

Emigrants often had to raise or lower their emptied wagon over walls of house-sized boulders, as in this painting by Harold Von Schmidt.

oirs, "I cannot express. I strapped on my blankets and dried beef, shouldered my gun, and began to retrace my steps to the cabin."

There were books in the cabin, and Moses "used to often read aloud, for I longed for some sound to break the oppressive stillness. For the same reason, I would talk aloud to myself. At night I built large fires and read by the light of the pine knots as late as possible, in order that I might sleep late the next morning, and thus cause the days to seem shorter."

Moses taught himself how to trap coyotes, foxes, and crows for food. "I had just coffee enough for one cup, and that I saved for Christmas." He was rescued in February and walked out of the mountains on snowshoes. Moses reached California's Sacramento Valley on March 1, 1845, exactly a year to the day he had left Missouri.

In November of 1846, the Donner Party reached a high mountain meadow in the Sierra Nevada. Snow fell, slowing their travel. Virginia Reed wrote: "We journeyed on . . . looking up with fear towards the mountains. . . . Despair drove many nearly frantic. Each family tried to cross the mountains but found it impossible."

The Donner Party had no choice but to camp in the mountains for the winter. They retreated to Alder Creek, about 6,500 feet in elevation, and to what is now called Donner Lake, near Moses Schallenberger's old cabin. Some families moved into Moses' cabin; others quickly built log cabins roofed with animal hides or put up tents. Before long, snow covered the simple cabins and nearly caved in the tents.

Virginia later wrote about "the long sleepless nights, the cold dark days we passed in that Cabin under the snow. . . . We used to sit and talk together and some times almost forget oneselfs for a while. We had a few books, I read them over and over. I read the 'Life of Daniel Boone' while there."

After running out of food, members of the Donner Party boiled and ate strips of animal hides that had served as rugs, blankets, and wall coverings. They gnawed on cow bones. Virginia recalled that her family killed and ate Cash, the family dog. One by one, members of the Donner Party died of cold and starvation. Sometime during that hard winter, the survivors began to roast and eat the flesh of those who had died.

The first group of rescuers arrived in February and started leading twenty-three people toward California. Virginia wrote: "We were out of the snow, could see the blessed earth and green grass again. No more dragging over the snow, when we were tired, so very tired. . . ."

Some mountain streams had bridges over them, which made travel easier for later pioneers. In winter, many of the high-elevation lakes and streams were buried under snow and ice.
(DENVER PUBLIC LIBRARY, WESTERN HISTORY COLLECTION)

Decades later, crossing the mountains was still treacherous. Here, in the 1880s, mule-drawn freight wagons carry supplies over the mountains to the growing western population.
(Denver Public Library, Western History Collection)

Her little sister and brother, Patty and Tommy, were too weak to hike out. At Donner Lake, where Patty turned nine on February 26, 1847, no one celebrated.

Another rescue group arrived and headed out with seventeen people, including Patty and Tommy. Patty brought Dolly, her small wooden doll, hidden in her clothes. Some children had to be carried. A powerful snowstorm lashed the mountains for two days and two nights. A five-year-old boy died during one night, huddled next to Patty.

Of the original eighty-seven members of the Donner Party, thirty-nine died on the trail west, at Donner Lake or Alder Springs, or after being rescued. Fifteen were children.

A few years later, Sallie Hester reached the mountains in California. She wrote: "We arrived at the place where the Donner Party perished. . . . Two log cabins, bones of human beings and animals, tops of the trees being cut off the depth of snow, was all that was left to tell the tale of that ill-fated party, their sufferings and sorrow."

They crossed the summit of the Sierra Nevada and began the descent into California. Sallie wrote in her journal about their "tedious march with pine knots blazing in the darkness and the tall, majestic pines towering above our heads. We could not ride—roads too narrow and rocky—so we trudged along, keeping pace with the wagons as best we could."

On October 6, 1849, after a five-month-long trip from St. Joseph, Missouri, they reached their destination in California. Sallie wrote: "Strangers in a strange land—what will the future be?"

Chapter Fourteen

THE EVER-CHANGING TRAIL AND TIMES

After gold was discovered in California, the trail west became a highway. Between 1850 and 1860, more than 200,000 people followed the Platte River route. Most of them were going to California.

Not everyone made it to the end of the trail. Sometimes people turned around for home. Poor grass and lack of water caused some travelers to become turnarounds. Others gave up if their stock was lost or stolen, or they changed direction after hearing about the high numbers of cholera deaths on the trail.

Lucy Ann Henderson reached Oregon but left her little sister Salita in a trailside grave. Catherine Sager buried both her parents. About ten thousand graves—many of them unmarked—lined the routes.

Some young people, like Moses Schallenberger, almost died in the mountains but reached their destinations. Virginia and Patty Reed, with the Donner Party, were also among those rescued. Safe in California, Virginia wrote her cousin back home:

I take this oppertunity to write to you to let you now that we are all Well at presant and hope this letter may find you all well to. . . . We are all very well pleased with Callifornia partuculary with the climate let it be ever so hot a day thare is all wais cool nights it is beautiful Country it is mostley in vallies it aut to be a beautiful Country to pay us for our trubel getting there.

A mismatched team of horse, oxen, mule, and cow pulls the wagon of these weary travelers into Baker City in Oregon Territory.
(Oregon Historical Society/ M. M. Hazeltine)

For Sarah Ide, many things went wrong, like when the family's favorite milk cow died in the California mountains. But Sarah stayed enthusiastic and wrote: "To me the journey was a pleasure trip, so many beautiful wild flowers, such wild scenery, mountains, rocks and streams—something new at every turn, or at least every day!"

After reaching California, twelve-year-old Elizabeth Keegan described her trip in a long letter to her brother and sister in St. Joseph,

Members of this 1867 wagon train stop at the plaza in Santa Fe, New Mexico. They may have gone on to California, Oregon, or some other final destination farther west.
(MUSEUM OF NEW MEXICO/ NICOLAS BROWN)

Missouri. "Dec. 12th 1852. My Dear Sister and Brother Our journey across the plains was tedious in the extreme We were over four months coming it is a long time to be without seeing any signs of civilization."

Sixteen-year-old John McWilliams left his family in Illinois to join California's gold rush. He came west in a wagon with three other boys from his hometown. New arrivals like John saw men and a few women washing the dirt from stream banks, looking for gold. The four friends may have pulled out their pans and tried to wash out some gold, too. John later wrote:

We had shovels and picks with us, which we had brought across the plains. But we didn't just know how to set to work, and were pretty well down at the mouth, for the California gold diggings of which we had thought so much, didn't look like a bit as we thought they would. In my imagination I thought I was going to dig gold out by the bucket-full.

When Charley True reached California in 1859, he didn't meet a lot of rich miners. "We found many deserted log cabins formerly occupied by miners and prospectors." Near the town of Placerville, he saw his first group of young Chinese men hard at work, digging for gold.

Pioneers usually arrived in Oregon's Willamette Valley at the start of the rainy season. They were tired; so were their animals. It was hard to build a home in the mud. Some families ended up spending their first winter in their covered wagon. Jesse Applegate recalled his first indoor

Daguerreotype of a miner's cabin. The covered wagon, minus its wheels, made a perfect extra room. A wooden yoke leans against the canvas cover.
(MATTHEW R. ISENBURG COLLECTION)

meal in the Willamette Valley, at the home of a missionary, and the wonderful smell of frying bacon.

Marion Russell never reached California. Her mother was robbed of her money and jewels during their trip in 1852 on the Santa Fe Trail. When the family reached Albuquerque, New Mexico, they had to leave the train. They found a house and Marion's mother took in boarders to pay the rent.

The first Mormon arrivals to the Great Salt Lake Valley had pushed aside knee-high sagebrush and planted late crops. They laid out streets, built temporary homes, and dug irrigation canals to divert streams and rivers to the valley. It was just the beginning. About seventy thousand

Pioneers often took apart their wagons and reused the valuable lumber to build a simple cabin. (NATIONAL ARCHIVES)

Mormons traveled west. Salt Lake City became their home, but non-Mormons continued to stop there for supplies, especially during California's gold rush years. Over the years, the Mormons built grist mills and sawmills. There were ironworks and tanneries, and, by 1853, companies that manufactured cloth and pottery. It wasn't easy, recalled Annie Cannon. "We had lots of trials but the Lord made the back equal to the burden."

Altogether, about forty thousand young people, like John McWilliams, Moses Schallenberger, Catherine Sager, John Brier, and Jesse Applegate came west during the great overland migration between 1840 and 1870. With their families, they built homes and started towns in Oregon, California, Utah, and many other places throughout the West.

These newly settled pioneers were helping to open up the country from the Atlantic to the Pacific Ocean. As a result, the country was changing.

In the 1860s, the Pony Express, a horseback mail delivery service,

After traveling for months, Mormon families saw the Great Salt Lake in the distance as they descended from the mountains. Painting by William Henry Jackson.
(Scotts Bluff National Monument)

stretched between St. Joseph, Missouri, and Placerville, California, following parts of the trails. Many of the riders were teenagers. They were lighter in weight and could ride farther than most men. The Pony Express lasted only about eighteen months. In 1861, telegraph poles were strung the entire length of the route. Messages could go from coast to coast in seconds, instead of being left on a buffalo skull or carried by a galloping horse and rider.

The Civil War began in the spring of 1861. In the western mining camps, work continued as usual. In 1862, Congress authorized the start of a transcontinental railroad to link the East with the West.

That same year, President Abraham Lincoln signed the Homestead Act, which opened public land for settlement. Farmers, ranchers, and railroad companies took another look at land in the middle regions of the United States. Anyone who headed a household and was twenty-one could claim up to 160 acres by living on the land, building a home on it, and farming it for five years. Starting in 1862, farmers, newly arrived immigrants, single women, and former slaves settled on this "free land." Eventually, ten percent of the area of the United States would be claimed and settled under this act. For the Indians, their vast open spaces were quickly disappearing all the way west to the Pacific Ocean.

During the Civil War, many men joined the military; some were stationed at frontier forts. But thousands of other men migrated west rather than go to war. And American settlers whose families were torn apart by the Civil War often headed west to start over.

After the Civil War, work on the transcontinental railroad picked up. Thousands of young men came to build the railroad. There were ex–Civil War soldiers and former slaves. Mormons and Native Americans worked side by side. There were many Irish immigrants, but some men came from Mexico, Germany, and Great Britain. Others arrived from China. Workers blasted tunnels through the mountains and built bridges over rivers. As the bones of slaughtered buffalo whitened on the prairie nearby, the ground was gradually covered with wooden ties upon which the train tracks would be laid.

In 1869 the Central Pacific and Union Pacific Railroads completed construction of the railroad line between Omaha, Nebraska, and Sacramento, California, a total of 1,775 miles of track. The last four spikes—two gold, one silver, and the fourth a blend of gold, silver, and iron—were set in place on May 10, 1869, at Promontory Summit, Utah.

The mass wagon migration of children and adults that took place between 1840 and 1870 was over. Now it took eight days to cross the

Railroads began to replace covered-wagon travel after the completion of the transcontinental railroad line in 1869. The wagons pictured here were carrying supplies for the railroad construction effort. They met this train as it traveled toward Promontory Summit, Utah.
(DEPARTMENT OF SPECIAL COLLECTIONS, STANFORD UNIVERSITY LIBRARIES)

continent instead of four to six months. Other kinds of wheels were replacing wagon wheels.

By the 1880s, most of the mountain men were dying off. Pioneer men and women were busy as farmers and business people. With the coming of the railroad, farmers' crops could go east by train. And all kinds of goods could be sent west. Businesses started up along the train stops. Before long, there were towns, and some of these grew into cities. But some pioneers, or their children, were still restless.

A cowboy sits astride his fast, sturdy pony, with lasso in hand. Horse and cowboy worked as a team to move the herd along the trail. (NATIONAL ARCHIVES)

About forty thousand young men became cowboys. Some five thousand of them were African American. Many were Spanish American. There were also a few cowgirls. Soon cowboys and cattle replaced wagons on the trails. By 1885, nearly half of the western land was devoted to raising cattle. Millions of cattle grazed on the open land, and then they were driven to railroad shipping towns. These cattle drives lasted several months or more.

Cowboys pushed herds north from Texas to railheads in Kansas, Nebraska, and Colorado. Large herds grazed on Montana and Wyoming grass before they moved south to a railroad. At the end of the trail, the cattle were loaded on railroad cars and shipped east to slaughterhouses. Soon there were numerous cattle trails. One, called the Chisholm Trail, stretched from San Antonio, Texas, to Abilene, Kansas.

The buffalo herds were all but gone. After the coming of the explorers, mountain men, and then the emigrants, the various Indian tribes could no longer freely roam the prairies, mountains, and deserts west of the Mississippi River. Some tribes nearly died out because of disease, while others lost men in battles. Tribes and people scattered. Cultures vanished. For the native peoples, a way of life ended.

Wagon wheel ruts are visible today in many places. Some angle across the open land; others are permanently etched through stone. Many of the names carved on Independence Rock and other sites are still there. Fort Laramie, Joseph Smith Historic Center, Scotts Bluff, the Whitman Mission, and Sutter's Fort are some of the historic places open to visitors. At the edge of highways, there are markers for the Lewis and Clark Trail, the Oregon Trail, the California Trail, the Mormon Trail, and the Santa Fe Trail.

Treasures continue to be discovered. A few years ago, a salvage worker unearthed a colorful English tin box in a northern California dump. He found a worn, leather-bound diary and a pair of baby shoes

Oregon Trail ruts in Nebraska.
(Oregon Historical Society)

inside. The small book had belonged to sixteen-year-old Lizzie Charlton. It was her diary when she traveled west in 1866. On July 31, somewhere in Oregon, and when it was undoubtedly hot on the trail, Lizzie wrote about "a very lonesome day too. . . . It was the lone some est day I most ever saw." It was her last entry. Lizzie settled in Oregon. The baby shoes probably belonged to Belle, Lizzie's youngest child.

Undiscovered journals and letters, in trunks, dressers, or desk drawers—or even in dumps—promise to tell us more about what it was like for children as well as adults during the great migration west.

NUMBER OF TRAVELERS
WHO MIGRATED WEST BY WAGON TRAIN

YEAR	ESTIMATED NUMBER OF TRAVELERS*	YEAR	ESTIMATED NUMBER OF TRAVELERS*
1841	100	1854	20,000
1842	200	1855	7,000
1843	1,000	1856	12,000
1844	2,000	1857	6,000
1845	5,000	1858	7,500
1846	1,000	1859	20,000
1847	2,000	1860	20,000
1848	4,000	1861	10,000
1849	40,000	1862	20,000
1850	65,000	1863	20,000
1851	10,000	1864	40,000
1852	70,000	1865	20,000
1853	35,000	1866	25,000

Estimated Total   462,800

*Estimates vary from source to source. Most counts were kept at various forts along the trail. This chart is from Merrill Mattes's *Platte River Narratives*. The same information is posted at the National Historic Oregon Trail Interpretive Center in Baker City, Oregon.

Epilogue and Sources

IN THE PROMISED LAND

Here is a brief reminder of where some children started from and when, along with details of what happened to them after they reached the "promised land."

Most young people I've written about, except for Moses Laird and John Minto, came with their families as well as other relatives, or with neighbors from their hometowns. Martha Gay, Thomas Chambers, John Roger James, and Mary Ellen Todd made it to Oregon, as did Adrietta Hixon and Jesse Applegate.

Sophia Goodridge, and her little brother, George, settled in Utah. Annie Cannon reached Utah and lived to be ninety years old. Mary Field lived over one hundred years and wrote that "my mind is clear and my memory is good of things both past and present." After being in Utah for two years, Edwin Pettit moved to California. He married, fathered fourteen children, and died at the age of seventy-eight.

Maria Elliott, Jasper Hill, Kate McDaniel, Elisha Perkins, Jasper Lawn, and Billy Walker traveled over the Sierra Nevada into California. Maggie Hall crossed the southern deserts into California.

Mary Burrell was nineteen when she arrived in California. Lucy Knight grew up in Oregon. Eighteen-year-old Eugenia Zieber settled in Oregon City, at the end of the Oregon Trail. All three women married and died young, leaving behind husbands and small children. It is not clear why they died so early in life. Some death notices mention consumption, which we call tuberculosis today.

Various pioneers, in writing their memoirs, only wanted to record that special time when they crossed the United States as children. They wanted to share the experience with their grandchildren, knowing it was also an important part of our history. They didn't write much, if anything, about their jobs, spouses, or children.

The following is what happened to some of the other young pioneers and where I found the diary or memoir excerpts used in this book. Refer to the For Further Reading and Research section for details about each source.

Mary Ackley: At the age of ten, Mary left for California with her family in 1852. Her mother died of cholera while they traveled along the Platte River. After five months, the family reached their destination near Marysville, California. Mary later wrote: "I must pay tribute to our wheel oxen, Dick and Berry, who drew the family wagon all the way across the plains. They were gentle, kind, patient and reliable. I loved them."

More of Mary's recollections are in Werner's *Pioneer Children on the Journey West* and Faragher's *Women and Men on the Overland Trail.*

John Bidwell: John traveled from Missouri to California. In 1844 he became a naturalized Mexican citizen, which entitled him to receive a large land grant. Then he acquired a second grant. In 1848, he made a rich gold strike. After California became a state, he was a state senator, and then he was elected to the United States Congress. He donated part of his land to establish the town of Chico in northern California.

John and his wife, Annie, gave land for the California State University of Chico. He died in 1900.

His account appears in Werner and Hewitt's *Eye-Witnesses to Wagon Trains West.*

Benjamin Bonney: With his parents, Benjamin and his six brothers and sisters left Illinois for Oregon on April 12, 1845. En route, his family decided to settle in California. They crossed the Sierra Nevada and camped by a mountain stream for three days to rest the teams. "It was October," Benjamin recalled, "and the water was low. In many places there were sand and gravel bars. On one of these gravel bars I saw what I thought was wheat, when I picked it up I found it was heavy." The pea-sized nugget he had plucked from the stream bed was pure gold. The discovery was kept secret and his family planned to return in the spring to pan for gold. During the spring of 1846, they decided to move to Oregon instead. Two years later gold was discovered at Sutter's Mill in California, and the gold rush began. Benjamin never returned to California. He later told his grandchildren "about the plains being dark, with . . . buffalo, about the Indians and the mining camps. . . . Those days are gone forever, and the present generation can never know the charm and romance of the old west."

John Bidwell.
(CALIFORNIA STATE LIBRARY)

The sources for Benjamin's recollections, first published in the *Oregon Historical Quarterly* in 1923, are Werner, Lockley's *Voices of the Oregon Territory,* Kimball's *Stories of Young Pioneers in Their Own Words,* and Hatch's *Pathways of America: The California Gold Rush Trail.*

John Brier: John, his brothers, and his parents left Wisconsin in the spring of 1849 and reached Los Angeles the following March. Following in his father's footsteps, John became a minister and lived in California.

The quote I used came from Werner.

Elisha Brooks: Elisha, age eleven, set out in 1852 to go from Michigan to California with his mother, four brothers, and one sister. They planned to join their father in the gold fields. It was a hard, long trip to California. At the end of the trail, Elisha worked in the mines and delivered milk "on horseback in cans slung in canvas bags." He eventually became a high school teacher, then a school administrator, and raised a family in Ben Lomond, California.

Elisha's quotes are from his memoir, *A Pioneer Mother of California*, published in San Francisco (1922), and from Kimball.

Helen Carpenter.
(THE HUNTINGTON LIBRARY)

Helen Carpenter: Helen, a nineteen-year-old bride of four months, and her husband, with a party of three families, left Kansas on May 26, 1857. Helen wrote about the pleasures and difficulties of the trip. She and her husband settled in northern California.

Helen's quotes are used courtesy of The Huntington Library. Read more from her diary in Myres's *Ho for California!*

Lizzie Charlton: Lizzie traveled from Iowa to Oregon in 1866, when she was sixteen. She married in November of 1867 and had three children. Lizzie was buried next to her youngest child, Belle, in Lebanon, Oregon. Belle's granddaughter, Natheel, lived in Monterey, California, and died there in 1990. The dump where the tin box holding the diary and baby shoes was discovered is nearby.

Lizzie's quotes are used courtesy of the National Frontier Trails Center archives in Independence, Missouri.

Sarah Cummins: Sarah and her family left Missouri for Oregon in 1845. Sarah was sixteen, newly married, and pregnant. Instead of going down the Columbia River by boat, Sarah joined her husband and, with

A page from Lizzie Charlton's diary, July 20 to July 22, 1866.

(NATIONAL FRONTIER TRAILS CENTER)

others, helped drive the animals over the mountains. It was an adventure she never forgot. Sarah suffered from frostbite and climbed Oregon's Mt. Hood. At the summit, she wrote, "I sat down, lost in thought and admiration of the beautiful and wonderful view that opened before my eyes."

Sarah's words come from Faragher, Horn's *The Pioneers* and Ruth Barnes Moynihan's "Children and Young People on the Overland Trail," published in the *Western Historical Quarterly* (volume 6, 1975).

Eliza Donner (Houghton): Both Eliza's parents died in the mountains during the winter of 1846–47. Eliza and her sisters were rescued and taken to California. Eliza married at the age of eighteen and was the mother of six children. Her husband was a senator, representing California.

Read more about Eliza in Werner.

Lucy Ann Henderson (Deady): It took her family about seven months to go from Missouri to Oregon in 1846. They were out of food and their cattle were nearly exhausted when they reached the end of the trail. The first winter, the family lived on boiled wheat and peas. Lucy Ann's father built a log cabin in 1848 but hurried off to find gold in California. He came back with some money, so Lucy Ann and her sister were able to go to school. The next summer, "I was fifteen . . . and in those days the young men wonder[ed] why a girl was not married if she was still single and . . . sixteen. That summer [Matthew] Deady . . . came by," and Lucy Ann and Matthew were married. Her husband had come west in 1849 and taught school. Later he became a district judge and then was elected to the House of Representatives of Oregon Territory. Lucy Ann had five children. She was eighty-eight when she talked about her life, saying that her "memories of the trip are very vivid." Her sister Olivia, who was born on the trail, had ten children and lived to be ninety-two.

Lucy Ann's recollections appear in Schlissel's *Women's Diaries of the Westward Journey,* Kimball, Lockley's *Conversations with Pioneer Women,* and her own memoir, *Crossing the Plains to Oregon in 1846,* published by the Oregon Pioneer Association (1928).

Sallie Hester (Maddock): Sallie traveled west in 1849. On October 5, 1871, she was married in a quiet home wedding, probably in San Jose, California. The newlyweds moved to the mining town of Eureka, Nevada, where Sallie's husband was an assayer. Her final diary entry reads: "Dear Journal, I give thee up. No more jottings down of gay and festive scenes—the past is gone and the future is before me."

Read more from Sallie's diary in Werner, Levy's *They Saw the Elephant: Women in the California Gold Rush* and Holmes's *Covered Wagon Women: Diaries and Letters from the Western Trails (volume 1: 1840–1849).*

Harriet Adelle Hitchcock (Lucas): To keep track of her journey from Pennsylvania to the gold fields in Colorado, thirteen-year-old Harriet wrote a diary during her trip. She later married a minister and raised a family. She died in Berkeley, California, in 1928.

Harriet's diary is quoted in Holmes (volume 8: 1862–1865) and Robert L. Munkres's "Emigrant Pets" in *The Tombstone Epitaph.*

Sarah Ide (Healy): Sarah's father, like many men of the time, couldn't stay settled long. He and his wife moved their six children from Kentucky to Ohio, and then to Illinois. In 1845, the family set off for Oregon. But at Fort Hall, the family met Caleb Greenwood and decided to go to California. Sarah and her family reached Sacramento, California, on October 25, 1845.

Sarah's 1888 remembrances are in Werner and Lewis's *Pioneers of California* and are used by permission of The Bancroft Library at the University of California, Berkeley.

Elizabeth Keegan: Elizabeth arrived in California in 1852 with her mother, a servant girl, and a hired man. She rode horseback the entire way. Her brother and sister came west two years later. Little is known about her, but census reports state that she died in 1907, when she was in her sixties.

Quotes from Elizabeth's 1852 letter about her trip are used courtesy of the California State Library, California History Section, and also appear in Werner and Holmes (volume 4: 1852).

Nancy Kelsey: In 1841, Nancy became the first white woman to reach California in an overland emigrant party. Interviewed for a newspaper when she was elderly, Nancy said: "I have enjoyed riches and suffered the pangs of poverty. I have seen U.S. General Grant when he was little known: I have baked bread for General Fremont and talked to Kit Carson; I have run from bear."

Werner, Levy, and Lewis are my sources for Nancy's quotes.

Edward Lenox: Edward was part of a large Missouri-based company that migrated to Oregon in 1843. He was the oldest of seven children, and his father was the captain of the wagon train.

Edward's quote is from Kimball.

Eliza Ann McAuley (Egbert): Eliza Ann wrote about her journey west in 1852 in a little five-by-seven-inch red book. After running out of ink, she made ink from plants along the way. She managed to write eighty-eight pages. Two years after arriving in California, she married a forty-niner. They lived on a ranch and raised seven children. Eliza Ann died at the age of eighty-three.

Each of Eliza Ann's quotes is from "Mother's Diary: the Record of a Journey Across the Plains in '52," MS 645 in the North Baker Research Library Manuscript Collections, and they are used by permission of the California Historical Society. Parts of her journal are quoted in Holmes (volume 4: 1852), Levy, Williams's *Wagon Wheel Kitchens: Food on the Oregon Trail*, and Collings's "The Oregon Trail."

John McWilliams: John traveled west from Illinois to California with friends at the age of sixteen. He was nearly ninety years old when he completed his recollections.

His quotes come from Werner and Kimball.

Martha Ann Morrison (Minto): Martha made the trip to Oregon in 1844 at the age of thirteen. Two years later, she married John Minto, who had come west the same year. She recalled that we "had just one stew kettle . . . to make coffee, or bread, or to fry meat. . . . We had just two sheets and one little bit of a bed with a few feathers in it. . . . I cut up the sheets to make shirts for my husband and then we had none. We slept [on] a pile of straw." Within eighteen months, Martha and John were the parents of two children; they would eventually raise eight in all. John was a sheep rancher, an author, and a state legislator.

The quotes I used are from Schlissel.

Rebecca Nutting (Woodson): In 1850, Rebecca reached Nevada City, California, where her family built a wooden house and took in boarders. Her mother and sisters cooked for paying boarders all winter. About a year later, Rebecca was married. "Father went and got the [preacher] to come and marry us—Father moved away the next morning after I was married leaving me a girl of a little more than 16 years to cook and do the house work for 20 men sometimes more." By the time she was eighteen, Rebecca had two children and lived in a mining camp full of men.

Quotes from Rebecca's 1909 memoirs, fifty-nine years after her trip, are used courtesy of the California State Library, California History Section, and can also be found in Schlissel.

Patty Reed's small doll survived her trip and is in a museum at Sutter's Fort State Historic Park in Sacramento, California. (Nikki Pahl photo)

Olive Oatman (Fairchild): After being rescued, Olive wrote and spoke about her time with the Indians. She married John Fairchild, and they lived in Texas until her death in 1903. She never saw her Mohave Indian friends again.

The quote I used comes from Werner.

Patty Reed (Lewis): At the age of eight, Patty left Illinois and reached California the following year. She married Frank Lewis in 1856, when she was eighteen, and had eight children.

Virginia Reed (Murphy): After being rescued from the mountains, Virginia lived in California for the rest of her life. She was married at the age of sixteen to John M. Murphy, who had traveled west with Moses Schallenberger in 1844–45. They had nine children.

Quotes are from Werner, Holmes (volume 1: 1840–1849), and Hatch.

Marion Russell: In 1865, Marion married a soldier at Fort Union, New Mexico. They had nine children. Marion died in 1936, at the age of ninety-one, after being hit by a car.

Read more about Marion's trip on the Santa Fe Trail in her memoir, *Land of Enchantment,* the source of the quotes included here. My own adaptation of Marion's trip, *Along the Santa Fe Trail,* provides additional information.

Catherine Sager (Pringle): After the attack on the Whitman Mission, Catherine was rescued. The surviving Sager sisters were separated and raised by different families. On October 25, 1851, sixteen-year-old Catherine married Clark Pringle. They lived near Salem, Oregon, and had eight children. Catherine died in 1910 at the age of seventy-five.

Thompson's *Shallow Grave at Waiilatpu: The Sagers' West,* Duncan's *The West: An Illustrated History for Children,* and West's *Growing Up*

Three of the surviving Sager daughters at the fiftieth anniversary of the Whitman Massacre in 1897. Left to right: Elizabeth Helm, Catherine Pringle, and Matilda Delaney. (NORTHWEST AND WHITMAN COLLEGE ARCHIVES)

with the Country: Childhood on the Far Western Frontier are the quote sources, but most come from Catherine's own published recollections about her 1844 trip.

Moses Schallenberger: Moses traveled west from Missouri in 1844–45 with his sister and her husband. Moses eventually settled in San Jose, California. After his sister and her husband died, he raised their son. He married in 1856, fathered five children, and lived to be eighty-three.

The source for Moses's quotes is Stewart's *The California Trail.*

Abigail Jane "Jenny" Scott (Duniway): Jenny migrated from Illinois to Oregon in 1852, at the age of seventeen. She was one of nine surviving children and the second oldest. Her father gave her the task of keeping the journal. Jenny lived in Oregon and raised six children. She had her own newspaper, *The New Northwest,* and fought for women's property and voting rights.

Thanks to Professor Ruth Moynihan, author of many articles and books, including *Rebel for Rights: The Life of Abigail Scott Duniway,* for her insights on the Scott family. Read more about each sister in Holmes (volume 5: 1852), the source for my Scott quotes.

Mary Frances "Fanny" Scott (Cook): At the age of nineteen, Fanny was the oldest Scott daughter. Her father assigned her to cook. She married an Oregon farmer and was a prohibitionist.

Catherine Amanda "Kit" Scott (Coburn): Kit was thirteen at the time of the trip and responsible for the care of the two youngest children. Willie, the baby in the Scott family, died on the trail.

Rachel Taylor: On July 22, 1853, Rachel celebrated her fifteenth birthday on the Oregon Trail. She and her family went from Illinois to the Rogue River Valley in southern Oregon. Off and on during her adult years, Rachel was a schoolteacher. She married twice and had five children.

Holmes (volume 6: 1853–1854) is the source of Rachel's quotes.

Samuel Tetherow: Sam was just nine in 1845 when the family started for Oregon from Missouri. His father was the captain of their wagon train. There were ten children in the Tetherow family. A brother, David, died during the trip. Sam recalled that in Oregon, his father traded an ox named Brindle for a square mile of land near what is now called Dallas. Sam became a farmer, married twice, and raised four children.

Sam is quoted in Faragher.

Susan Thompson (Lewis Parrish): Susan left Independence, Missouri, in May 1850. The wagon train reached Tucson, Arizona, on January 8, 1851, the day she turned eighteen. Susan's family settled at El Monte, California, a station on the stagecoach road between San Bernardino and Los Angeles. In 1853, she married and moved to Los Angeles. Lorenzo Oatman lived with them for a while and tried to find his missing sisters, Olive and Mary Ann. After Olive was rescued, she lived with Susan. "In time we erased the tattoo marks from her face, but we could not erase the wild life from her heart," Susan recalled.

Susan wrote her reminiscences in 1860, and her quotes are from Levy and Werner.

Charley True: Charley traveled west when he was sixteen but wrote his memoirs when he was in his seventies. From southern Minnesota, he headed west on May 1, 1859, with his parents, brother, and two sisters. In California, he was a schoolteacher and principal. He spent most of his life in California and raised a son and two daughters.

The quotes are from *The Overland Memoir of Charles Frederick True: A Teenager on the California Trail, 1859,* published by the Oregon-California Trail Association (1993).

Mary Eliza Warner: Mary Eliza traveled from Illinois to California with her parents, her brothers, and a little sister in 1864. The family settled on a cattle ranch in the Sierra Nevada.

The quote appears in Schlissel.

Charles E. Young: Influenced by the writing of Horace Greeley, editor of the *New York Tribune,* who had advised young men to go west and grow up with the country, Charles and a friend did just that. Charles didn't mention his age in his memoirs, only that he was a boy. In July 1865, at the close of the Civil War, he started west, first by train to Atchison, Kansas. Then he was hired by a wagon train to help cook for twenty-five men.

Charles's *Dangers on the Trail in 1865: A Narrative of Actual Events,* published in Geneva, New York, is the source of his quotes.

My sources for other quotes in the text follow. Full bibliographical information can be found starting on page 179.

Jesse Applegate: Werner's *Pioneer Children on the Journey West,* Rucker's *The Oregon Trail and Some of Its Blazers,* Horn's *The Pioneers,* and Hewitt's *Eyewitnesses to Wagon Trains West*
Jim Beckwourth: DeVoto's *The Year of Decision: 1846*
Mary Burrell: Holmes's *Covered Wagon Women* (volume 6: 1853–1854)
Annie Cannon: Kimball's *Stories of Young Pioneers in Their Own Words*
Thomas Chambers: Faragher's *Women and Men on the Overland Trail*
William Clark: Bakeless's *The Journals of Lewis and Clark*
Maria Elliott: Werner
Mary Field: Kimball
Martha Gay (Masterson): Masterson's *One Woman's West*
Sophia Goodridge: Kimball
Maggie Hall: Werner
Jasper Smith Hill: Werner
Adrietta Hixon: Schlissel's *Women's Diaries of the Westward Journey*
John Roger James: Williams's *Wagon Wheel Kitchens*

Lucy Knight's mother, Amelia: Schlissel

Moses Laird: Blackwood's *Life on the Oregon Trail*

Jasper Henry Lawn: Judy Allen's "Children on the Overland Trails," published in the *Overland Journal* (volume 12: 1994)

Meriwether Lewis: Peters's *Seven Trails West*

James Marshall: Duncan's *The West: An Illustrated History for Children*

Kate McDaniel: Allen and Hewitt's *Eyewitnesses to Wagon Trains West*

Joe Meek: Duncan

John Minto: Faragher and Thompson's *Shallow Grave at Waiilatpi*

Elisha Perkins: Schanzer's *Gold Fever!*

Edwin Pettit: Kimball

James Polk: Blackwood

William Thompson: Faragher

Mary Ellen Todd: Faragher and Schlissel

Billy Walker: Bruff's *Gold Rush*

Daniel Webster: Duncan

Sarah Yorke: Collings's "The Oregon Trail"

Eugenia Zieber: Holmes (volume 3: 1851), used courtesy of the Salem Art Association/Bush House Museum in Salem, Oregon

Young people spelled their names in many ways, married, and had birthdays on the trail, and so ages and names sometimes changed en route. Reminiscences were often written decades later and might be subject to faulty memory. I take full responsibility for any errors or omissions. They are certainly unintentional.

Chronology

1801–1809	Thomas Jefferson is president of the United States.
1803	The United States buys five hundred million acres from France, called the Louisiana Purchase.
1804–1806	Lewis and Clark Expedition.
1812	Fur trader Wilson Price Hunt discovers South Pass through the Rocky Mountains.
1821	Missouri becomes a state.
	September, Mexico wins independence from Spain.
1821–1822	William Becknell, a Missouri farmer, takes trade goods to Santa Fe in New Mexico Territory and sells them there. His trip opens up commercial trade on the Santa Fe Trail.
1827	Fort Leavenworth, a military fort, is established on the Missouri River to protect settlers and emigrants west of the Missouri River.
1830	Joseph Smith publishes the *Book of Mormon* and founds what becomes the Church of Jesus Christ of Latter-day Saints.
1834	Fort William in present-day Wyoming (later called Fort John and Fort Laramie) and Fort Hall in present-day Idaho are built.
1836	March 2, Texas claims independence from Mexico.
	Missionaries Marcus and Narcissa Whitman settle in Oregon Country and attempt convert western Indians to Christianity.
1837	Economic panic grips the United States.
1839	John Sutter starts his colony, New Helvetia, on the American River in California.
1841	Bidwell-Bartleson Party goes overland by wagon train.
1843	November 6, Peter H. Burnett's company is the first to arrive in Oregon City by wagon.
1845	Texas becomes a state.
1845–1849	James Polk is president of the United States.
1846	February 4, Mormons are driven from Nauvoo, Illinois.
	May 13, war begins between Mexico and the United States.
	May 13, Great Britain cedes Oregon Country to the United States.
	Iowa becomes a state.

1847	Survivors of the Donner-Reed Party are rescued in the Sierra Nevada.
	July 24, Brigham Young, leading the Mormon Pioneer Company, reaches the Great Salt Lake Valley in the future state of Utah.
	November 29, Indians kill Marcus and Narcissa Whitman and others at their mission.
1848	Construction begins on Fort Kearny (first called Fort Childs) on the Platte River.
	January 24, James Marshall discovers gold at Sutter's Mill in California.
	February 2, the Treaty of Guadalupe Hidalgo is signed in Mexico, ending the Mexican War.
1849	The California gold rush begins.
1850	California becomes a state.
1851	Fort Union is established on the Mountain Branch of the Santa Fe Trail.
1859	Oregon becomes a state.
1860	The first Pony Express mail goes from St. Joseph, Missouri, to Sacramento, California, and back.
	Abraham Lincoln is elected president.
1861	April 12, Civil War begins.
	Kansas becomes the thirty-fourth state.
	October 24, the first transcontinental telegraph line is completed between New York and California.
	November 24, the Pony Express makes its final run to Sacramento, California.
1862	Congress passes the Homestead Act, granting 160 acres of public land to settlers after five years of residence.
1864	Nevada becomes a state.
1865	April 9, the Civil War ends.
1867	Nebraska becomes a state.
1869	May 10, the Central Pacific and Union Pacific Railroads join at Promontory Summit, Utah, in the Golden Spike Ceremony, linking the west with the East Coast.
1876	Colorado becomes a state.
1889	Montana and Washington become states.
1890	Idaho and Wyoming become states.
	Bureau of Census officially declares the frontier closed.
1896	Utah becomes a state.
1912	New Mexico becomes a state.

Acknowledgments

Without the diaries and reminiscences of hundreds of young pioneers, this book would not have happened. Numerous others—authors, illustrators, mapmakers, and photographers—have also helped make the West come alive. Thanks to all of you, including those who have passed on to the "Happy Hunting Grounds," as my late father used to say. My house is filled with your books, drawings, and photographs.

Deep thanks go to my expert readers, Cathy Luchetti, author of many books, including *Children of the West;* JoAnn Levy, who wrote *They Saw the Elephant: Women in the California Gold Rush* and other books; and Ruth Moynihan, professor and author of *Rebel for Rights: The Life of Abigail Scott Duniway.*

In my research for this book, I explored cemeteries, forts, monuments, historical sites, historical societies, museums, ghost towns, and libraries from St. Louis, Missouri, to Fort Clatsop, Washington.

Thank you to the staff at Brigham Young University's Harold B. Lee Library; Bush House Museum in Salem, Oregon; California Historical Society; California State Library; Colorado Historical Society; Frontier National Trails Center in Independence, Missouri; Kansas State Historical Society; Library of Congress; National Archives; Nebraska State Historical Society; Oregon Historical Society; Sharlot Hall

Museum in Prescott, Arizona; Smithsonian Institution; and Strong Museum in New York.

I especially appreciate the assistance of Bill Lindemann at the California State Parks; Coi Drummond-Gehrig at the Denver Public Library, Western History Department; Peter Blodgett at The Huntington Library; Ellen Thomasson at the Missouri Historical Society; Eleanor Gillers at the New-York Historical Society; Dean Knudsen at Scotts Bluff National Monument; Larry Dodd at Whitman College; Leslie Shores at University of Wyoming's American Heritage Center; Chris Brewer; Matthew R. Isenburg; the late Peter Palmquist; and so many others. Thanks also to Gretchen, Lauren, and Katy Zane.

I'd like to acknowledge Howard Allen, whose technical skills made archival photographs come to life; Jennifer B. Greene, my editor, for her gentle but on-target editing; Kathy Shepler, Aurora School librarian in Oakland, California, who let me borrow her school's trail books for an entire summer; and my husband, Bill Wadsworth, for being my research partner, editor, and trail compadre.

Thank you to the countless assistants, volunteers, docents, and historians who helped me at every place I visited. I loved meeting individuals and families "on the trail," who shared their experiences and gave me directions to their favorite spots.

This is a book that doesn't reach "the end of the trail." I look forward to meeting more "rut nuts," exploring new-to-me parts of each trail, and reading journals that have yet to be uncovered!

For Further Reading and Research

There are thousands of books, articles, videos, and games about the western migration. My many sources include the published and unpublished diaries, memoirs, and letters of the young people who traveled west in covered wagons. I found them in periodicals and historical society publications dating back to the late 1800s. Some are posted on the Internet.

My father's and grandfather's research books, some published as early as 1835, gave me invaluable access to the literature, thoughts, and beliefs of that time period. I did not list most of these books in the bibliography because they are out of print and hard, if not impossible, to find. Here are some of the books and articles I used.

SPECIAL INTEREST

Blumberg, Rhoda. *The Great American Gold Rush*. New York: Bradbury Press, 1989. A fascinating look at the California gold rush.

Calabro, Marian. *The Perilous Journey of the Donner Party*. New York: Clarion Books, 1999. A detailed account of the saga of this famous wagon train.

Cobblestone magazine. "The Oregon Trail" (December 1981), "Mountain Men" (December 1991), and "The Mormon Pioneer Trail" (May 1997). Each issue is a great source of information.

Duncan, Dayton. *The West: An Illustrated History for Children*. Boston: Little, Brown and Company, 1996. Based on the PBS series, this book has many illustrations and easy-to-read information.

Freedman, Russell. *Children of the Wild West*. New York: Clarion Books, 1983. A good look at children and their roles as America moved west.

Goldsmith, Connie. *Lost in Death Valley: The True Story of Four Families in*

California's Gold Rush. Brookfield, Connecticut: Twenty-First Century Books, 2001. Read more about the Brier family and others as they crossed Death Valley in 1849–50.

Holmes, Kenneth L., editor. *Covered Wagon Women: Diaries and Letters from the Western Trails, 1840–1890*. 11 volumes. Lincoln: University of Nebraska Press, Bison Books, 1995–2000. This series of eleven books is an invaluable resource.

Ichord, Loretta Frances. *Skillet Bread, Sourdough, and Vinegar Pie: Cooking in Pioneer Days*. Brookfield, Connecticut: Millbrook Press, 2003. With tasty pioneer recipes for today's chefs.

Lavender, David. *The Santa Fe Trail*. New York: Holiday House, 1995. A concise look at this trail.

Levy, JoAnn. *They Saw the Elephant: Women in the California Gold Rush*. Norman: University of Oklahoma Press, 1992. This excellent book shows the role of women during the California gold rush.

Luchetti, Cathy. *Children of the West*. New York: W. W. Norton and Company, 2001. With wonderful photographs.

Myres, Sandra L., editor. *Ho for California!* San Marino, California Huntington Library Press, 1980. Includes the complete diary of Helen Carpenter.

Peavy, Linda, and Smith, Ursula. *Frontier Children*. Norman: University of Oklahoma Press, 1999. A well-presented look at children on the western frontier with great pictures and lively text.

Peters, Arthur King. *Seven Trails West*. New York: Abbeville Press, 1996. An informative book on the seven main trails to the West. Excellent illustrations.

Wadsworth, Ginger, adapter. *Along the Santa Fe Trail: Marion Russell's Own Story*. Morton Grove, Illinois: Albert Whitman & Company, 1993. In Marion Russell's own words, this is the story of her first trip on the Santa Fe Trail.

Werner, Emmy E. *Pioneer Children on the Journey West*. Boulder, Colorado: Westview Press, 1995. A wonderful resource on children who came west during the mid-1800s.

SELECTED BIBLIOGRAPHY

Adult Books/Articles

Armitage, Susan, and Jameson, Elizabeth, editors. *The Women's West*. Norman: University of Oklahoma Press, 1987.

Bakeless, John. *The Journals of Lewis and Clark*. New York: Signet Classic, 2002.

Bell, Marianne. *Frontier Family Life: A Photographic Chronicle of the Old West*. New York: Barnes & Noble, 1998.

Blevins, Win. *Dictionary of the American West*. Seattle, Washington: Sasquatch Books, 2001.

Billington, Ray Allen, and Ridge, Martin. *Westward Expansion*. New York: Macmillan Company, 1982.

Blodgett, Peter J. *Land of Golden Dreams: California in the Gold Rush Decade, 1848–1858.* San Marino, California: Huntington Library Press, 1999.

Bruff, J. Goldsborough. *Gold Rush: The Journals, Drawings and Other Papers of J. Goldsborough Bruff.* Edited by Georgia Willis Reed and Ruth Gaines. New York: Columbia Press, 1949.

Collings, Kit. "The Oregon Trail." *Pioneer Trails West.* Edited by Don Worcester. Caldwell, Idaho: Caxton Printers, 1985, 131–150.

Danneberg, Julie. *Amidst the Gold Dust: Women Who Forged the West,* Golden, Colorado: Fulcrum Publishing, 2001.

DeVoto, Bernard. *The Year of Decision: 1846.* Boston: Houghton Mifflin Company, 1942.

———. *Across the Wide Missouri.* Boston: Houghton Mifflin Company, 1947.

Faragher, John Mack. *Women and Men on the Overland Trail.* New Haven: Yale University Press, 1979.

Flaherty, Thomas, and Hicks, Jim, editors. *The Women.* New York: Time-Life Books, 1978.

Hewitt, James, editor. *Eye-Witnesses to Wagon Trains West.* New York: Charles Scribner's Sons, 1973.

Holliday, J. S. *The World Rushed In: The California Gold Rush Experience.* New York: Simon & Schuster, 1981.

Horn, Huston. *The Pioneers.* New York: Time-Life Books, 1974.

Jackson, William Henry. *Time Exposure.* Tucson, Arizona: Patrice Press, 1994.

Jeffrey, Julie Roy. *Converting the West: A Biography of Narcissa Whitman.* Norman: University of Oklahoma Press, 1991.

———. *Frontier Women: The Trans-Mississippi West, 1840–1880.* New York: Hill and Wang, 1979.

Ketchum, Liza. *The Gold Rush.* Boston: Little, Brown and Company, 1996.

Lavender, David. *The Overland Migrations: Settlers to Oregon, California and Utah.* Washington, D.C.: Publications of the National Park Service (n.d.).

———. *Westward Vision: The Oregon Trail.* New York: McGraw-Hill Book Company, 1963.

Lewis, Donovan. *Pioneers of California.* San Francisco: Scottwall Associates, 1993.

Lockley, Fred. *Conversations with Pioneer Women.* Eugene, Oregon: Rainy Day Press, 1981.

———. *Voices of the Oregon Territory.* Eugene, Oregon: Rainy Day Press, 1981.

Luchetti, Cathy. *Women of the West.* Berkeley: Antelope Island Press, 1982.

Masterson, Martha Gay. *One Woman's West: Recollections of the Oregon Trail and Settling the Northwest Country 1836–1916.* Edited by Lois Barton. Eugene, Oregon: Spence Butte Press, 1986.

Mattes, Merrill. *The Great Platte River Road: The Covered Wagon Mainline Via Fort Kearny to Fort Laramie.* Lincoln: Nebraska State Historical Society, 1969.

May, Christina Rae. *Pioneer Clothing on the Oregon Trail.* Pendleton, Oregon: Drigh Sighed Publications, 1998.

Morgan, Dale, editor. *Overland in 1846: Diaries and Letters of the California-Oregon Trail*. Volume 1. Lincoln: University of Nebraska Press, 1963.

Moynihan, Ruth Barnes. *Rebel for Rights: The Life of Abigail Scott Duniway*. New Haven, Connecticut: Yale University Press, 1983.

———. "Children and Young People on the Overland Trail." *Western Historical Quarterly* 6 (1975): 279–294.

———, Armitage, Susan, and Dichamp, Susan Fischer, editors. *So Much to Be Done*. Lincoln: University of Nebraska Press, 1990.

Nunis, Doyce B., Jr. *The Bidwell-Bartleson Party: 1841 California Emigrant Adventure*. Santa Cruz, California: Western Tanager Press, 1991.

Paden, Irene D. *The Wake of the Prairie Schooner*. New York: Macmillan Company, 1947.

Palmer, Rosemary Gudmundson. *Children's Voices from the Trail: Narratives of the Platte River Road*. Spokane, Washington: Arthur H. Clark Company, 2002.

Parkman, Francis. *The Oregon Trail*. Boston: Little, Brown and Company, 1928.

Peavy, Linda, and Smith, Ursula. *Pioneer Women: The Lives of Women on the Frontier*. Norman: University of Oklahoma Press, 1998.

Riley, Glenda, and Etulain, Richard W., editors. *By Grit & Grace: Eleven Women Who Shaped the American West*. Golden, Colorado: Fulcrum Publishing, 1997.

Rucker, Maude A. *The Oregon Trail and Some of Its Blazers*. New York: W. Neale, 1930.

Russell, Marion. *Land of Enchantment: Memoirs of Marion Russell Along the Santa Fe Trail*. Albuquerque: University of New Mexico Press, 1954.

Schlissel, Lillian. *Women's Diaries of the Westward Journey*. New York: Schocken Books, 1982.

———, Gibbons, Byrd, and Hampsten, Elizabeth. *Far from Home: Families of the Westward Journey*. New York: Schocken Books, 1989.

Seagraves, Anne. *High Spirited Women of the West*. Hayden, Idaho: Wesanne Publications, 1992.

Stewart, George. *The California Trail*. New York: McGraw-Hill Book Company, 1962.

———. *Ordeal by Hunger: The Story of the Donner Party*. New York: Ace Books, with Houghton Mifflin Company, 1936.

Stone, Irving. *Men to Match My Mountains: The Opening of the Far West 1840–1900*. New York: Doubleday & Company, 1956.

Stratton, Joanna L. *Pioneer Women: Voices from the Kansas Frontier*. New York: Simon & Schuster, 1981.

Thompson, Erwin N. *Shallow Grave at Waiilatpu: The Sagers' West*. Portland: Oregon Historical Society, 1969.

West, Elliott. *Growing Up with the Country: Childhood on the Far Western Frontier*. Albuquerque: University of New Mexico Press, 1989.

Williams, Jacqueline. *Wagon Wheel Kitchens: Food on the Oregon Trail*. Lawrence: University Press of Kansas, 1993.

Wilson, Elinor. *Jim Beckwourth: Black Mountain Man and War Chief of the Crows.* Norman: University of Oklahoma Press, 1981.

Juvenile Books

Ammon, Richard. *Conestoga Wagons.* New York: Holiday House, 2000.

Bial, Raymond. *Frontier House.* Boston: Houghton Mifflin Company, 1993.

Blackwood, Gary. *Life on the Oregon Trail.* San Diego: Lucent Books, 1999.

Bunting, Eve. Illustrated by Greg Shed. *Dandelions.* San Diego: Voyager Books/ Harcourt, 1995.

Freedman, Russell. *Indian Chiefs.* New York: Holiday House, 1987.

———. *Buffalo Hunt.* New York: Scholastic, 1988.

Hatch, Lynda. *Pathways of America: The California Gold Rush Trail.* Carthage, Illinois: Good Apple, 1994.

Herb, Angela M. *Beyond the Mississippi: Early Westward Expansion of the United States.* New York: Dutton Children's Books, 1996.

Kimball, Violet T. *Stories of Young Pioneers in Their Own Words.* Missoula, Montana: Mountain Press Publishing Company, 2000.

Kurtz, Jane. *I'm Sorry, Almira Ann.* New York: Henry Holt and Company, 1999.

Lavender, David. *Snowbound: The Tragic Story of the Donner Party.* New York: Holiday House, 1996.

Leland, Dorothy Kupcha. *Sallie Fox: The Story of a Pioneer Girl.* Davis, California: Tomato Press, 1995.

Levine, Ellen. *. . . If You Traveled West in a Covered Wagon.* New York: Scholastic, 1986.

Littlefield, Holly. *Children of the Trail West.* Minneapolis: Carolrhoda Books, 1999.

Miller, Brandon Marie. *Buffalo Gals: Women of the West.* Minneapolis: Lerner Publications Company, 1995.

Murphy, Virginia Reed. *Across the Plains in the Donner Party.* Edited by Karen Zeinert, New Haven, Connecticut: Shoe String Press, 1996.

Place, Marian T. *Westward on the Oregon Trail.* New York: American Heritage Publishing Co., 1962.

Rau, Margaret. *The Ordeal of Olive Oatman: A True Story of the American West.* Greensboro, North Carolina: Morgan Reynolds, 1997.

Sandler, Martin W. *Pioneers: A Library of Congress Book.* New York: HarperCollins Books, 1994.

Schanzer, Rosalyn. *Gold Fever! Tales from the California Gold Rush.* Washington, D.C.: National Geographic Society, 1999.

———. *How We Crossed the West: The Adventures of Lewis and Clark.* Washington, D.C.: National Geographic Society, 1997.

Silverman, Jerry. *Singing Our Way West: Songs and Stories of America's Westward Expansion.* Brookfield, Connecticut: Millbrook Press, 1998.

Stefoff, Rebecca. *The Oregon Trail in American History*. Springfield, New Jersey: Enslow Publishers, 1997.

———. *Children of the Westward Trail*. Brookfield, Connecticut: Millbrook Press, 1996.

Terry, Michael. *Daily Life in a Plains Indian Village 1868*. New York: Clarion Books, 1999.

Index

Note: Page numbers in **bold** type refer to illustrations.